PARAKEETS

Books LLC®, Wiki Series, Memphis, USA, 2011. ISBN: 9781158076673. www.booksllc.net
Copyright: http://creativecommons.org/licenses/by-sa/3.0/deed.en

Table of Contents

Broad-tailed parrots
Australian Ringneck 1
Blue Bonnet (bird) 2
Bourke's Parrot 2
Budgerigar 3
Budgerigar colour genetics 9
Crimson Rosella 10
Eastern Ground Parrot 13
Eastern Rosella 13
Golden-shouldered Parrot 15
Green Rosella 15
Mulga Parrot 16
Night Parrot 17
Northern Rosella 17
Orange-bellied Parrot 18
Pale-headed Rosella 19
Paradise Parrot 20
Pezoporus 21
Psephotus 21
Red-capped Parrot 22
Red-rumped Parrot 22
Rock Parrot 23
Rosella 23
Scarlet-chested Parrot 24
Swift Parrot 25
Turquoise Parrot 26
Western Ground Parrot 27
Western Rosella 28

Conures
Maroon-bellied Parakeet 29

Parakeets
Mani the parakeet 29

Introduction

Purchase of this book entitles you to a free trial membership in the publisher's book club at www.booksllc.net. (Time limited offer.) Simply enter the barcode number from the back cover onto the membership form. The book club entitles you to select from hundreds of thousands of books at no additional charge. You can also download a digital copy of this and related books to read on the go. Simply enter the title or subject onto the search form to find them.

Each chapter in this book ends with a URL to a hyperlinked online version. Type the URL exactly as it appears. If you change the URL's capitalization it won't work. Use the online version to access related pages, websites, footnotes, tables, color photos, updates. Click the version history tab to see the chapter's contributors. Click the edit link to suggest changes.

A large and diverse editor base collaboratively wrote the book, not a single author. After a long process of discussion and debate, the chapters gradually took on a neutral point of view reached through consensus. Additional editors expanded and contributed to chapters striving to achieve balance and comprehensive coverage. This reduced the regional or cultural bias found in many other books and provided access and breadth on subject matter otherwise little documented.

Australian Ringneck

The **Australian Ringneck** (*Barnardius zonarius*) is a parrot native to Australia. Except for extreme tropical and highland areas, the species has adapted to all conditions. Traditionally, two species were recognised in the genus *Barnardius*, the **Port Lincoln Parrot** (*Barnardius zonarius*) and the **Mallee Ringneck** (*Barnardius barnardi*), but the two species readily interbred at the contact zone and are now considered one species. Currently, four subspecies are recognised, each with a distinct range.

In Western Australia, the Ringneck competes for nesting space with the Rainbow Lorikeet, an introduced species. To protect the Ringneck, culls of the lorikeet are sanctioned by authorities in this region. Overall, though, the Ringneck is not a threatened species.

Description

The subspecies of the Australian Ringneck differ considerably in colouration. It is a medium size species around 33 cm (11 in) long. The basic colour is green, and all four subspecies have the characteristic yellow ring around the hindneck; wings and tail are a mixture of green and blue.

B. z. semitorquatus, Perth, Western Australia

The *B. z. zonarius* and *B. z. semitorquatus* subspecies have a dull black head; back, rump and wings are brilliant green; throat and breast bluish-green. The difference between these two subspecies is that *B. z. zonarius* has a yellow abdomen while *B. z. semitorquatus* has a green abdomen; the latter has also a prominent crimson frontal band that the former lacks (the intermediate shown in the box has characteristics of both subspecies). The two other subspecies differ from these subspecies by the bright green crown and nape and blush cheek-patches. The underparts of *B. z. barnardi* are turquoise-green with an irregular orange-yellow band across the abdomen; the back and mantle are deep blackish-blue and this subspecies has a prominent red frontal band. The *B. z. macgillivrayi* is generally pale green, with no red frontal band, and a wide uniform pale yellow band across the abdomen.

The calls of the Mallee Ringneck and Cloncurry Parrot have been described as "ringing", and the calls of the Port Lincoln Ringneck and Twenty-eight have been described as "strident". The name of the Twenty-eight Parrot is an onomatopoeic derived from its distinctive 'twentee-eight' call.

Taxonomy and naming

The Australian Ringneck was first described by the English naturalist George Shaw in 1805. It is a Broad-tailed parrot and related to the rosellas of the genus *Platycercus*; it has been placed in that genus by some authorities, including Ferdinand Bauer.

Currently, four subspecies of Ringneck are recognised, all of which have been described as distinct species in the past: (As of 1993, the Twenty-eight and Cloncurry Parrot were treated as subspecies of the Port Lincoln Parrot and the Mallee Ringneck, respectively).

The classification of this species is still debated, and recent molecular research has found that all subspecies are very closely related. Several other subspecies have been described, but are considered synonyms with one of the above subspecies. *B. z. occidentalis* has been synonimised with *B. z. zonarius*. Intermediates exist between all subspecies except for between *B. z. zonarius* and *B. z. macgillivrayi*. Intermediates have been associated with land clearing for agriculture in southern Western Australia.

Behaviour

The Australian Ringneck is active during the day and can be found in eucalypt woodlands and eucalypt-lined watercourses. The species is gregarious and depending on the conditions can be resident or nomadic. In trials of growing hybrid eucalypt trees in dry environments parrots, especially the Port Lincoln Parrot, caused severe damage to the crowns of the younger trees during the research period between 2000–3.

Feeding

This species eats a wide range of foods that include nectar, insects, seeds, fruit, and native and introduced bulbs. It will eat orchard-grown fruit and is sometimes seen as a pest by farmers.

Breeding

Breeding season for the Northern populations starts in June or July, while the central and southern populations breed from August to February, but this can be delayed when climatic conditions are unfavourable. The nesting site is a hollow in a tree trunk. Generally four or five white oval eggs are laid measuring 29 mm x 23 mm, although a clutch may be as few as three and as many as six. Fledgling survival rates have been measured at 75%.

Conservation

Although the species is endemic, the species is considered not threatened, but in Western Australia, the Twenty-eight subspecies (*B. z. semitorquatus*) gets locally displaced by the introduced Rainbow Lorikeets that aggressively compete for nesting places. The Rainbow Lorikeet is considered a pest species in Western Australia and is subject to eradication in the wild.

In Western Australia, a license is required to keep or dispose of more than four Port Lincoln Ringnecks. All four subspecies are sold in the Canary Islands and in Australia, and they are traded via the CITES convention. The sale of the Cloncurry Parrot is restricted in Queensland. The Australian Ringneck can suffer from Psittacine Beak and Feather Disease, which causes a high nestling mortality rate in captivity.
Source (edited): "http://en.wikipedia.org/wiki/Australian_Ringneck"

Blue Bonnet (bird)

The **Blue Bonnet** (*Northiella haematogaster*) is an Australian parrot, the only member of the genus *Northiella*. Its habitat includes open woodland, scrub, riverine forest, spinifex, and farmlands in the eastern half of the continent, with a smaller race being found in the Western Australian Nullarbor region.

This species grows up to 27–35 cm in length and the sexes are similar in appearance. They are usually seen in pairs or small groups feeding along roads. They breed between July and December producing 4 to 7 white eggs.

It is a moderately common species in the wild though not so in captivity due to its duller colouring and pugnacious behaviour.

The genus name commemorates the Australian ornithologist Alfred John North.
Source (edited): "http://en.wikipedia.org/wiki/Blue_Bonnet_(bird)"

Bourke's Parrot

The **Bourke's Parrot** (*Neopsephotus bourkii*, formerly known as *Neophema bourkii*), also known as the **Bourke's Parakeet** or "Bourkie", is a small parrot originating in Australia and the only species in its genus *Neopsephotus*. This species is sometimes placed in the genus *Neophema* and there is an ongoing discussion about the proper taxonomic placement of this species. It is a grass parrot approximately 19 cm long and weighing around 45 grams. It is named after General Sir Richard Bourke, Governor of New South Wales from 1831 to 1837.

Description

Wildtype (natural coloured) Bourke's Parakeet display a basically brown overall colouration with pink abdomen, pinkish breast & a blue rump. The legs are dark-brown, with zygodactyl toes. The bill is yellowish-brown. The adult male has a blue forehead while the adult female has a little or no blue on the forehead.

Breeding

The Bourke's Parrot has a clutch of 3 to 6 eggs, which are incubated by the female for 18–19 days, with the chicks fledging at about 4 weeks of age. The female also feeds and tends to the chicks by herself. While the female Bourke's Parrot is incubating the eggs, and also while she is feeding the chicks in the nest, she is fed by the male Bourke's Parrot.

Eulo Bore, SW Queensland, Australia

At Flying High Bird Habitat, Queensland. The adult male has blue on its forehead.

Pair of wild Bourke's parrots, SW Queensland, Australia.

Source (edited): "http://en.wikipedia.org/wiki/Bourke%27s_Parrot"

Budgerigar

The **Budgerigar** (/ˈbʌdʒərɪɡɑr/), also known as **Common Pet Parakeet** or **Shell Parakeet** (*Melopsittacus undulatus*), informally nicknamed the **budgie**, is a small, long-tailed, seed-eating parrot, and the only species in the Australian genus *Melopsittacus*. Wild budgerigars are found throughout the drier parts of Australia, where the species has survived harsh inland conditions for the last five million years. Naturally green and yellow with black, scalloped markings on the nape, back, and wings, breeders have created a rainbow of blues, whites, and yellows, greys, and even forms with small crests. Budgerigars are popular pets around the world due to their small size, low cost, ability to mimic human speech and playful nature.

The budgerigar is closely related to the lories and the fig parrots. Although budgerigars are often, especially in American English, called *parakeets*, this term refers to any of a number of small parrots with long, flat tails.

Etymology

Alternative common names include Shell Parrot, Warbling Grass parakeet, Canary Parrot, Zebra parrot, Flight Bird, Scallop Parrot and the alternate spellings Budgerygah and Betcherrygah. Although more applicable to members of the genus *Agapornis*, the name Lovebird has been applied to them from their habit of mutual preening.

Several possible origins for the English name *budgerigar* have been proposed:

- A mispronunciation or alteration of Gamilaraay *gidjirrigaa* [ɡʲiɟiriɡaː], possibly influenced by the Australian slang word *budgery* "good". This is supported by the American Heritage Dictionary.
- A compound of *budgery*, "good" and *gar* "Cockatoo". This is supported by the Oxford English Dictionary. The word *budgery* itself, also spelt *boojery*, was formerly in use in Australian English slang meaning "good".

The Budgerigar was first described by George Shaw in 1805, and given its current binomial name by John Gould in 1840. The genus name *Melopsittacus* comes from Greek and means "melodious parrot". The species name *undulatus* is Latin for "undulated" or "wave-patterned". Gould noted that the term *Betcherrygah* was used by indigenous people of the Liverpool plains.

Traditionally, the budgerigar was thought to be the link between the genera *Neophema* and *Pezoporus* based on the barred plumage. However, recent phylogenetic studies using DNA sequences place the budgerigar very close to the lories (subfamily Loriinae) and the fig parrots (tribe Cyclopsittacini).

Anatomy and physiology

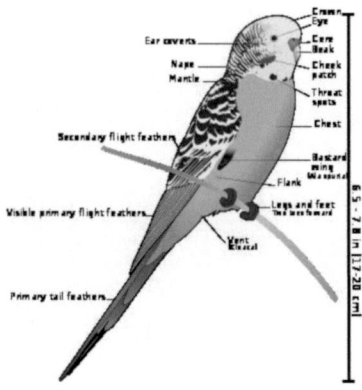

The anatomy of a male budgerigar.

Budgerigars in their natural-habitats of Australia average 18 cm (7 in) long, weigh 30–40 grams (1.1–1.4 oz), and display a light green body colour (abdomen and rumps), while their mantle (back and wing coverts) display pitch-black mantle markings (blackish in fledgelings and immatures) edged in clear yellow undulations. The forehead and face is yellow in adults but with blackish stripes down to the cere (nose) in young individuals until they change into their adult plumage around 3–4 months of age. They display small, purple patches (called cheek patches) and a series of three black spots across each sides of their throats (called throat-spots). The two outermost throat-spots are situated at the base of each cheek-patch. The tail is cobalt (dark-blue); outside tail feathers display central yellow flashes. Their wings have greenish-black flight feathers and black coverts with yellow fringes along with central yellow flashes, which only becomes visible in flight or when the wings are outstretched. Bills are olive grey and legs blueish-grey, with zygodactyl toes.

Budgerigars in their natural habitat in Australia are noticeably smaller than those in captivity. This particular parrot species has been bred in many other colours and shades in captivity (e.g. blue, grey, grey-green, pieds, violet, white, yellow-blue), although they are mostly found in pet stores in blue, green, and yellow. Like most parrot species, budgerigar plumage fluoresces under ultraviolet light. This phenomenon is possibly related to courtship and mate selection.

The upper half of their beaks is much taller than the bottom half and covers the bottom when closed. The beak does not protrude much, due to the thick, fluffy feathers surrounding it, giving the appearance of a downward-pointing beak that lies flat against the face.

The colour of the cere (the area containing the nostrils) differs between the sexes, being royal blue in males, pale brown to white (non-breeding) or brown (breeding) in females, and pink in immatures of both sexes (usually of a more even purplish-pink colour in young males). Some female budgerigars develop brown cere only during breeding time which later returns to the normal colour. Young females can often be identified by a subtle chalky whiteness that starts around the nostrils. Males that are either Albino, Lutino, Dark-eyed Clear or Recessive Pied (aka Danishpied aka Harlequin) always retain the immature purplish-pink cere colour their entire life.

Budgerigar flock in the wild (SW Queensland, Australia)

It is usually easy to tell the sex of a budgerigar over six months old, mainly by the cere colours, but behaviours and head shape also help indicate sex.

A mature male's cere is usually light to dark blue, but can be purplish to pink in some particular colour mutations (DarkEyedClears, Danishpieds aka Recessivepieds and Inos) which usually display much rounder heads. Males are typically cheerful, extroverted, highly flirtatious, peacefully social, and very vocal.

Females' ceres are pinkish as immatures and switch from being beigish or whitish outside breeding condition into brown (often with a 'crusty' texture) in breeding condition and usually display flattened back of heads (right above the nape region). Females are typically highly dominant and more socially intolerant.

Vision

Like many birds, budgerigars have tetrachromatic colour vision, but all four classes of cone cells operating simultaneously requires the full spectrum provided by sunlight. Additionally, budgerigars are known to see in the ultra-violet spectrum, which brightens their feathers to attract mates. The throat-spots in budgerigars reflect UV and can be used to distinguish individual birds.

Ecology

Female Budgerigar at Alice Springs Desert Park.

Budgerigars are nomadic birds found in open habitats, primarily in scrubland, open woodland, and grassland of Australia. The birds are normally found in small flocks, but can form very large flocks under favourable conditions. The species is extremely nomadic, and the movement of the flocks is tied to the availability of food and water. Drought can drive flocks into more wooded habitat or coastal areas. They feed on the seeds of spinifex, grass seeds, and sometimes ripening wheat.

Naturalised feral budgerigars have been recorded since the 1940s in the St. Petersburg, Florida, area of the United States, but are much less common now than they were in the early 1980s. Increased competition from European Starlings and House Sparrows is thought to be the primary cause of the population decline.

Aviculture

Pet budgerigars

The budgerigar is widely acknowledged as the most popular pet parrot in the world and possibly the most popular cage bird. It has been bred in captivity since the 1850s. Breeders have worked over the decades to produce a wide range of colour, pattern, and feather mutations, such as albino, blue, cinnamon-ino (aka lacewinged), clearwinged, crested, dark, greywinged, opaline, pieds, spangled, dilute (suffused), and violet.

'English Budgie' (left), as compared to 'wild-type' Budgerigars

Standard-type (aka *English* or "show") budgerigars are about twice as large as their wild-type counterparts. Their overall larger sizes and puffier head feathers give them a boldly exaggerated look. The eyes and beak can be almost totally obscured by these fluffy head feathers. English budgerigars are typically more expensive than wild-type birds and typically have a shorter life span of 7–9 years. Breeders of English Budgerigars often exhibit their birds at animal shows. Most captive budgerigars in the pet trade are similar in size and body conformation to wild budgerigars.

Budgerigars are intelligent and social animals and enjoy the stimulation of toys and interaction with humans, as well as with other budgerigars. A common behaviour is chewing material such as wood, especially for females. When a budgerigar feels threatened, it will try to perch as high as possible and may make itself appear thin by bringing its feathers close against its body.

Tame budgerigars can be taught to speak, whistle tunes, and play with humans. Both males and females sing and can learn to mimic sounds and words and do simple tricks. Both singing and mimicry are more pronounced and better perfected in males. Females rarely learn to mimic more than a dozen words. Males can easily acquire vocabularies ranging between a few dozen to a hundred words. Pet males, especially those kept alone, are generally the best speakers.

A flock of budgerigars in an aviary

In captivity, budgerigars live an average of five to eight years, but life-spans of 15–20 years have been reported. The lifespan depends on breed, lineage, and health, being highly influenced by exercise and diet.

Budgerigars enjoy chewing on anything they can find. Mineral blocks (ideally enriched with iodine), cuttlebone, and soft wooden pieces must be provided to pet birds to satisfy their desire to chew and to keep their beaks trimmed.

Budgerigars have been shown to cause "bird fancier's lung" in sensitive people, a type of hypersensitivity pneumonitis. This is primarily an issue with people keeping large numbers of budgerigars within a bird room.

Cage requirements

Male pet in a cage

Budgerigars are small but energetic. The absolute *minimum* size cage for one or two tame pet budgerigars that are allowed out for several hours a day is 45 centimetres (18 in) long by 45 centimetres (18 in) wide. However, larger cages and flights will be appreciated by these energetic little birds. An ideal cage is longer than high (since birds fly more horizontally than vertically) and would be at least 75 centimetres (30 in) long. The cage should not have bar spacing greater than 1 centimetre (0.4 in) between bars. Budgerigars are not particularly destructive birds, and spacious cages, while sometimes hard to find, are usually inexpensive.

Minimum size for 1 budgerigars — 45×45×45 cm (18×18×18 in) Volume = 91,125 cm (5,561 cu in)

Minimum size for 2 budgerigars — 75×45×45 cm (30×18×18 in) Volume = 151,875 cm (9,268 cu in)

Minimum size for 3 budgerigars — 80×45×50 cm (31×18×20 in) Volume = 180,000 cm (10,984 cu in)

Minimum size for 4 budgerigars — 85×45×63 cm (33×18×25 in) Volume = 240,975 cm (14,705 cu in)

Minimum size for 5 budgerigars — 90×45×75 cm (35×18×30 in) Volume = 303,750 cm (18,536 cu in)

Minimum size for 6 budgerigars — 100×45×80 cm (39×18×31 in) Volume = 360,000 cm (21,969 cu in)

Care should be taken when placing several female budgerigars together, as they can do serious harm to one another if they do not get along.

Food variety sold for parakeets. Millet is the primary ingredient in budgerigar pet mix.

Pet budgerigars eating fruit

Although budgerigars in their natural habitat eat mainly grass seeds, captive budgerigars feed on dry, sprouted, or soaked seeds. A diet of only dry seeds is inadequate for budgerigars. Avian veterinarians recommend pet birds' diets be supplemented with foods such as whole cereals and whole grains like amaranth, barley, couscous, flax, pasta, oat, quinoa, wheat, and rice; and certain edible flowers, including carnation, chamomile, chive, dandelion, day lily, eucalyptus, hibiscus, honeysuckle, impatiens, lilac, nasturtium, pansy, passion flower (*Passiflora*), rose, sunflower, tulip, and violet (but the foliage of some of these plants is poisonous to the birds). Occasionally and sporadically budgerigars may be fed amaranth leaves, beet leaves, carambola (starfruit), chards, parsley, spinach, and turnip leaves, but the high oxalic acid content of these foods may cause health problems.

- **Fruit** (except grapefruit, lemons, plums, and avocadoes, which are toxic): all Apple varieties, Banana, all Berries varieties, Oranges, Grapes, Kiwi, Mango, Melons, Nectarine, Papaya, Peach, all Pear varieties, Star-fruit. Pits and seeds from every Citrus and Drupe species must always be discarded as they are intoxicating. However, achenes and tiny seeds from pseudo and true Berries (Bananas, Blueberries, Elderberries, Eggplants, Persimmons, Pomegranates, Raspberries, Strawberries, Tomatoes) are all okay.
- **Legumes:** Almonds, Lentils, Peas, Nuts and Tofu.
- **Grain and/or Legume sprouts:** Adzuki beans, Alfalfa beans, Buckwheat, Lentils, Mungo beans, Pinto beans, Red Kidney beans, Sesame seeds, Sunflower seeds. Caution with only Lima and Navy beans' sprouts which are toxic.
- **Vegetables** (except uncooked potatoes, uncooked onions, mushrooms, and all members of the cabbage family): Carrots, corn, cucumber, fresh romaine Lettuce, green peppers, zucchini.
- **Pellets** specifically formulated for budgerigars, for Australian grass budgerigars and/or for small parrots are all healthy additions.
- Other fat-free, healthy and nutritious human foods.

Adding these foods provides additional nutrients and prevents obesity and lipomas, as can substituting millet, which is relatively low in fat, for higher-fat seed mixes.. Parrots and budgerigars learn mainly by mimicry and thus most adult budgerigars will be easily encouraged to try new foods by observing another bird eating the food, or by placing the new food on a mirror.

Parrot species (including budgerigars) are herbivores. Consequently, they should be fed plant-based diets that are ideally supplemented with vegetable proteins, for example, produced by a combination of any type of whole grain with any type of legume. Eggs (hard-boiled) are the only appropriately healthy source of animal protein, mostly for birds in either breeding, growing, moulting and/or recovering conditions. High levels of proteins (particularly animal proteins) are unhealthy for budgerigars and other Grass Parakeet species living under any alternate conditions (i.e. non-breeding, pets).

Alcohol, avocado, chocolate, caffeine, products containing lactose, garlic and onions present a danger of toxicosis and should not be fed.

Breeding

Head detail of a male Budgerigar.

Breeding in the wild generally takes place between June and September in northern Australia and between August and January in the south, although budgerigars are opportunistic breeders and respond to rains when grass seeds become most abundant. Budgerigars show signs of affection to their flockmates by preening or feeding one another. Budgerigars feed one another by eating the seeds themselves, and then regurgitating it into their flockmates' mouth. Populations in some areas have increased as a result of increased water availability at farms. Nests are made in holes in trees, fence posts, or even logs lying on the ground; the 4-6 eggs are incubated for 18–21 days, with the young fledging about 30 days after hatching.

In the wild, virtually all parrot species require a hollow tree or a hollow log as a nest site. Because of this natural behavior, budgerigars most easily breed in captivity when provided with a nest box. The eggs are typically 1 to 2 centimetres long and are plain white without any coloration. Female budgerigars can lay eggs without a male partner but these eggs are unfertilised and will not hatch. When the female is laying eggs her cere turns a crusty brown colour. A female budgerigar will lay her eggs on alternate days. After the first one, there is usually a two-day gap until the next. She will usually lay between four to eight eggs, which she will incubate (usually starting after laying her 2nd or 3rd) for about 21 days each. Female Budgerigar only leave their nests for very quick defecations and stretches once they've begun incubating and are by then almost exclusively fed by their mate (usually at the nest's entrance). Depending on the clutch size and the beginning of incubation, the age difference between the first and last hatchling can be anywhere from 9 to 16 days. Rarely female has the habit of eating the eggs in case of insecurity.

Breeding problems

Budgerigar on sale in a retail setting

Breeding difficulties arise for various reasons. Some chicks may die from diseases and attacks from adults. Other budgerigars (virtually always females) may fight over the nest box, attacking each other or a brood. Sometimes budgerigars (mainly males) are not interested in the opposite gender, and will not reproduce with them. Sometimes a flock setting—several pairs housed where they can see and hear each other—is necessary to stimulate breeding. Another problem may be the birds' beak being under lapped. This is where the lower mandible is above the upper mandible.

Most health issues and physical abnormalities in budgerigars are genetic. Care should be taken that birds used for breeding are active, healthy, and unrelated. Budgerigars that are related or who have fatty tumours or other potentially genetic health problems should not be allowed to breed. Parasites (lice, mites, worms) and pathogens (bacteria, fungi and viruses), are contagious and thus transmitted between individuals through either direct or indirect contact. Nestboxes should be cleaned between uses.

Splay leg, a relatively common problem in baby budgerigars – in which one of the budgerigar's legs is bent outward, preventing it from being able to stand properly and compete with the other chicks for food and can also lead to difficulties in reproducing in adulthood, results from young budgerigars slipping repeatedly on the floor of a nestbox. It is easily avoided by placing a small quantity of a safe bedding or wood shavings in the bottom of the nestbox. Alternatively, several pieces of paper may be placed in the box for the female to chew into bedding.

Development

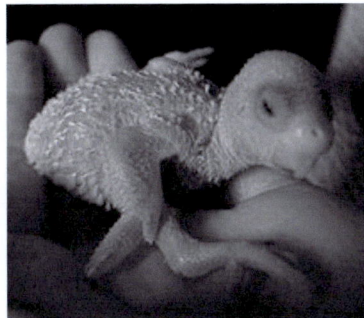

A baby chick 11 days old. (more)

Juvenile Budgerigars

The eggs will take about 18–20 days before they start hatching. The hatchlings are altricial – blind, naked, totally helpless, and their mother feeds them and keeps them warm constantly. Around 10 days of age, the chicks' eyes will open, and they will start to develop feather down. The appearance of down occurs precisely at the ages (around 9 or 10 days of age) for closed banding of the chicks. Budgerigar's closed band rings must be neither larger or smaller than 4.0 to 4.2 mm.

They develop feathers around 3 weeks of age. (One can often easily note the colour mutation of the individual birds at this point.) At this stage of the chicks' development, the male usually has begun to enter the nest to help his female in caring and feeding the chicks. Some budgerigar females, however, totally forbid the male from entering the nest and thus take the full responsibility of rearing the chicks until they fledge.

Depending on the size of the clutch and most particularly in the case of single mothers, it may then be wise to transfer a portion of the hatchlings (or best of the fertile eggs) to another pair. The foster pair must already be in breeding mode and thus either at the laying or incubating stages and/or rearing hatchlings.

As the chicks develop and grow feathers, they are able to be left on their own for longer and longer periods of time. By the fifth week, the chicks are strong enough that both parents will be comfortable in staying more and more out of the nest. The youngsters will stretch their wings to gain strength before they attempt to fly. They will also help defend the box from enemies mostly with their loud screeching. Young budgerigars typically fledge (leave the nest) around their fifth week of age and are usually completely weaned a week later. However, the age for fledging as well as weaning can vary slightly depending on whether it is the oldest, the youngest and/or the only surviving chick. Generally speaking, the oldest chick is the first to be weaned. But even though it is logically the last one to be weaned, the youngest chick is often weaned at a younger age than its older sibling(s). This can be a result of mimicking the actions of older siblings. Lone surviving chicks are often weaned at the youngest possible age as a result of having their parent's full attention and care.

Hand-reared Budgies may take slightly longer to wean than parent-raised chicks. Hand feeding is not routinely done with budgerigars, due to their small size, and the fact that young parent raised birds can be readily tamed.

Colour mutations

Adult females (top) display beige to brown ceres while adult males (bottom) typically have blue ceres or purplish-pink in Albinistic and recessive-pied varieties.

All captive budgerigars are divided into two basic series of colours; namely, white-based (i.e. blue, grey & white budgerigars) and/or yellow-based (i.e. green, greygreen & yellow budgerigars). There are presently at least 32 primary mutations in the budgerigar(including violet), enabling hundreds of possible secondary mutations (stable combined primary mutations) and colour varieties (unstable combined mutations).

Common Color Mutations: -Albino(all white, red eyes) -Lutinos(all yellow, red eyes) -Nomal sky blue(sky blue body, White head & crown, stripes on back) -Normal Cobalt(cobalt, blue body, white head & crown, stripes on back) -Normal mauve(a grayish mauve, white head head & crown, stripes on back) -Normal violet(violetish blue body, white head & crown, stripes on back) -Yellow faced blue(blue body, yellow head neck & crown, often stripes on back) -Opaline light green(light green body, yellow head neck & crown, stripes on back, not a mutation)

There are many more uncommon mutations

Mimicry

Male specimens of budgerigars are considered one of the top five talking champions amongst parrot species, alongside the African Grey Parrot, the Amazon parrot species, the Eclectus Parrot and the Ring-necked Parakeet.

A budgerigar named Puck holds the world record for the largest vocabulary of any bird, at 1,728 words. Puck, a male budgerigar owned by American Camille Jordan, died in 1994, with the record first appearing in the 1995 edition of Guinness World Records.

In 2001, recordings of a budgerigar called Victor got some attention from the media. Victor's owner, Ryan B. Reynolds of Canada, states that Victor was able to engage in contextual conversation and predict the future.

Though some believe the animal was able to predict his own death as was claimed, further study on the subject is difficult without the bird. The recordings still remain to be verified by scientific analysis. Critics argue that Victor's speech in the recordings is not coherent enough to be determined as spoken in context.

Source (edited): "http://en.wikipedia.org/wiki/Budgerigar"

Budgerigar colour genetics

Melopsittacus undulatus at Chai-Negev, Revivim, Israel.

The science of **budgerigar colour genetics** deals with the heredity of mutations which cause colour variation in the feathers of the species known scientifically as *Melopsittacus undulatus*. Birds of this species are commonly known by the terms 'budgerigar', 'budgerigar parakeet' or just 'budgie'.

Background

The Wildtype (natural-coloured or wild occurring) Budgerigar Parakeet's colour is called Lightgreen. The feathers of most Parrot species, including Budgerigars, contain both a black type of *melanin* named *eumelanin* along with a basic yellow pigment named psittacofulvin (psittacin for short). Some other Parrot species produces a third pigment named advanced-psittacin which enables colours & tones ranging from oranges, peaches, pinks to reds. When these feathers are exposed to a white light source, such as sunlight, only the blue part of the spectrum is reflected by the eumelanin granules. This reflected blue light passes through the yellow pigment layer, resulting in the green colouration known as *Lightgreen* in only the Budgerigar Parakeet &/or Green in any other naturally green coloured Parrot species.

The many colour variations of Budgerigars, such as Albino, Blue, Cinnamon, Clearwinged, the various Fallows, Grey, Greygreen, Greywing, Lutino, Mauve, Olive, Opaline, Spangled, Suffused, Violet... are the result of mutations that have occurred within specific genes. There are actually at least thirty-two known primary mutations established among Budgerigar Parakeets. These can combine to form hundreds of secondary mutations & colour varieties which may or may not be stable.

As is true with all animal species, colour mutations occur in captivity as do in the wild. This has been demonstrated when captive-bred Budgerigars have developed mutations that had only been previously recorded amongst wild populations.

Classification of mutations

Basic groups

Each of the thirty-two primary mutations belong to one of the four basic groups of mutations classified in parrot species genetics:

Because of albinism this budgerigar has virtually no eumelanin pigment. This, together with the Blue mutation which removes the yellow pigmentation, produces a nearly pure white colouration along with clear (orange) beak, pink feet/skin, white-tipped clear (pink) toe nails & red eyes.

- Albinism : where eumelanin is either partially or completely reduced in all body tissues & structures.
- Dilution : where eumelanin is partially reduced in only feathering.
- Leucism : where eumelanin is completely reduced from total or localized feathering.
- Melanism : where eumelanin is increased in the feathering.

Dominance relationship

These mutations are inherited through one of the following dominance relationships.
- autosomal-Co-Dominant (A-Co-D),
- autosomal-Complete-Dominant (A-C-D),
- autosomal-Incomplete-Dominant (A-I-D),
- autosomal-recessive (A-R),
- autosomal-Poly-Genic (A-P-G)
- Sex-Linked-recessive (S-L-R)

History

In the first few decades of the 1900s, especially in-between World War I and II, the keeping and breeding of the Budgerigar had become very popular all around the world. Consequently, various mutations occurred and were soon established during this period.

Time line

- **1870-75** The very first registered sudden captive-bred colour mutations were Suffused Green (aka Dilute Yellow), Greywinged Green and either one of the two types of Lutino (NSLino &/or SLino) mutations. All three occurred in aviaries in Great Britain or Europe. Of these three mutations, only the Suffused Green (aka Dilute Yellow) has survived. The latter was easily reproduced in great numbers and is nowadays very well established. The first Lutino mutation quickly vanished but it was re-established in Europe some time between 1931 and 1933.
- **1878-85** The Skyblue mutation suddenly occurred in continental Europe, most probably in Uccle, Belgium. Surprisingly, this variety was not imported in England until

1910.
- **1915** Single-Factored Dark-Green (aka Dark-Green) in France (where they were then commonly called 'Laurel' which is the French word for Bay (leaf &/or tree))
- **1916** Double-Factored Dark-Green (aka Olive) in France.
- **1918-28** Respectively, Greywinged Green and Greywinged Blue appeared in England and continental Europe.
- **1920**
  - Crest-Factor in Australia.
  - Suffused Blue (aka Dilute White) in England and France.
  - Single-Factored Dark_Blue (aka Cobalt) in France.
- **1921** Double-Factored Dark_Blue (aka Mauve) in France.
- **1930**
  - Single-Factored Violet-Green (aka Violet Factor) in Australia (and were then 1st commonly called 'Satin Green')
  - The first Clearwinged Green (Yellowinged) appeared, developed by H. Pier in Sydney.
- **1931**
  - Cinnamon in England, Australia & Germany.
  - An unknown type of Fallow in California, U.S.A. This soon vanished.
  - The Germanfallow in Germany, recently been genetically classified and identified as the Bronzefallow (aka Brownfallow).
  - A plum-eyed mutation, similar looking to Fallow mutations, occurred in England. This vanished or at least became very rare. This mutation was most probably the Brownwings, one of the rarest colour mutations of the species.
  - The first Albino specimens were produced in both England and continental Europe.
- **1932**
  - Three Fallow mutations occurred in England which became known as the Englishfallow. In Australia these have been genetically classified and identified as the Dunfallow or Greybrownfallow (aka Australianfallow). The Beigefallow or Palebrownfallow has been classified in South-Africa, but no reference seems to be available on this particular mutation.
  - The recessive Anti-dimorphic Pied (aka Danish Pied aka Harlequin) in Denmark.
  - The Australian (aka Banded) Pied in Australia.
- **1933**
  - Green Clearwinged (aka Yellow Wing) and Dominant Grey-Factor appear in Australia.
  - Both the NSL & the SL Lutino gene occurred in England and continental Europe.
  - Three Opaline mutations occurred. An Opaline Green hen was captured in the wild and sold to S. Terril in Adelaide. It was later-on reproduced and is most probably the ancestor of all Opaline specimens in Australia. Two sudden captive-bred Opaline mutations occurred in England and Holland.
- **1934** Recessive grey factor in England.
- **1935** The various Yellowfaced_Blue and Goldenfaced_Blue occurred in several locations.
- **1939-46** Clearflighted_Dutchpied in Belgium.
- **1948**
  - Texas Clearbodied (aka SL-Clearbody) in the U.S.A.
  - Dominant Clearbodied (aka Easley's Clearbodied) in the U.S.A.
  - The first Cinnamon-Ino (aka Lacewings) cross-over mutation was produced in Australia.
  - The first Dark-Eyed-Clear (DEC) variety was produced in Belgium by combining the ADM Pied (aka Danish/Recessive pied) with either one of the two Dutchpied varieties (Continental or Clearflighted).
- **1970-74** Single-Factored and Double-Factored Spangled specimens were produced in Australia.
- **1975** Saddleback specimens were produced in Australia.
- **1992** Blackface specimens make their first appearance in Holland.

Source (edited): "http://en.wikipedia.org/wiki/Budgerigar_colour_genetics"

Crimson Rosella

The **Crimson Rosella** (*Platycercus elegans*) is a parrot native to eastern and south eastern Australia which has been introduced to New Zealand and Norfolk Island. It is commonly found in, but not restricted to, mountain forests and gardens. The species as it now stands has subsumed two former separate species, The **Yellow Rosella** and the **Adelaide Rosella**. Molecular studies show one of the three red-coloured races, var. *nigrescens* is genetically more distinct.

Taxonomy

Swifts Creek, Victoria, Australia

Though described by Johann Friedrich Gmelin in *Systema Naturae* as *Psittacus elegans* in 1788, the Crimson Rosella had been described and named by John Latham in 1781 as the *Beautiful Lory*, and then *Pennantian Parrot*. However he didn't give it a Latin name until 1790, when he named it *Psittacus pennanti*. In 1854, it was placed in the genus *Platycercus* by Martin Lichtenstein in his *Nomenclator Avium Musei Zoologici Berolinensis*.

Today, the red-coloured races are generally known as the *Crimson Rosella*, with the alternate names *Red Lowry*, *Pennant's Parakeet*, *Campbell Parakeet*, *(Blue) Mountain Parrot*, *(Blue) Mountain Lowry* or just plain *Lowry* occasionally heard. Cayley reported that the first two alternate names were most common in the early part of the twentieth century. On Norfolk Island it is called simply *Red Parrot*.

The *Yellow Rosella*, also known by a variety of alternate common names including *Murrumbidgee Lowry*, *Murray Rosella*, *Swamp Lory* and *Yellow-rumped Parakeet*, was described as *Platycercus flaveolus* by John Gould, who gave it the last common name mentioned. It was reduced to subspecies status once hybridization was noted where ranges overlap, however some authorities maintain the hybridization is not widespread and hence preserve its specific status. This view is in the minority, however.

The name *Blue-cheeked Rosella* was proposed for the united species *elegans*, but was not generally taken up.

Description

Eating seeds from the ground. The feathers on the back have a scalloped pattern.

Juvenile showing green plumage

Platycercus elegans is a medium-sized Australian parrot at 36 cm (14 in) long, much of which is tail. There are five subspecies, three of which are actually crimson. The red is replaced by yellow in the case of var. *flaveolus* and a mixture of red, orange and yellow in the Adelaide Rosella.

Adults and juveniles generally show strikingly different colouration in southeastern populations, with predominantly greenish-olive body plumage on the juvenile, most persistent on the nape and breast. Juveniles are said to 'ripen' as they get older and turn from green to red. All races have blue cheeks and black-scalloped blue-margined wings and predominantly blue tail with predominantly red coloration. The Crimson Rosella's blue tail feathers are one of the favourite decorations of the Satin Bowerbird. The bill is pale grey and the iris dark brown.

There is very little sexual dimorphism in Crimson Rosellas. The most noticeable difference between genders is that males are up to 15% larger, and have a relatively larger and wider beak.

Crimson Rosella

P. elegans elegans, the nominate race of Victoria and eastern New South Wales. *P. elegans nigrescens*, occurring on Queensland's northeastern coast, and *P. elegans melanoptera* on Kangaroo Island. The main distinctions between these is size: *nigrescens* is the smallest of the three and *melanoptera* is the largest; both are slightly darker than the nominate race.

The juveniles of var. *nigrescens* lack the greenish immature plumage of the other subspecies of Crimson Rosella

Yellow Rosella

The Yellow Rosella, which lives along the Murray River, was reclassified (1968) as a subspecies, *P. elegans flaveolus*, of the Crimson as the two were found to interbreed where their ranges overlap. The main difference between the two is that those parts of the Crimson which are red are on the Yellow bright yellow.

Adelaide Rosella

The Adelaide Rosella of Adelaide and the surrounding area, was also thought to be a separate species, but is presently believed to be a hybrid swarm, having originated through interbreeding of the Crimson and Yellow Rosellas. Both of these still interbreed with the Adelaide Rosella where its range crosses theirs, and it exhibits variation in its plumage from dark orange-red in the south of its distribution to a pale orange-yellow in the north. Variants that are very close to the Yellow race are designated *subadelaidae*.

Distribution and habitat

Juvenile with prominent green plumage

Crimson Rosella

The Crimson Rosella occurs from southeastern South Australia, through Victoria and coastal New South Wales into Southeastern Queensland. A disparate population occurs in North Queensland.

It is common in coastal and mountain forests at all altitudes. It primarily lives in forests and woodlands, preferring older and wetter forests. They can be found in tropical, subtropical, and temperate rainforests, both wet and dry sclerophyllous forests, riparian forests, and woodlands, all the way from sea-level up to the tree-line. They will also live in human-affected areas such as farmlands, pastures, fire-breaks, parks, reserves, gardens, and golf-courses. They are rarely found in treeless areas. At night, they roost on high tree branches.

Behaviour

Almost all Rosellas are sedentary, although occasional populations are considered nomadic; no Rosellas are migratory. Outside of the breeding season, Crimson Rosellas tend to congregate in pairs or small groups and feeding parties. The largest groups are usually composed of juveniles, who will gather in flocks of up to 20 individuals. When they forage, they are conspicuous and chatter noisily. Rosellas are monogamous, and during the breeding season, adult birds will not congregate in groups and will only forage with their mate.

Feeding

Adult eating seeds from a basil plant in a garden in Canberra, Australia

Crimson Rosellas forage in trees, bushes, and on the ground for the fruit, seeds, nectar, berries, and nuts of a wide variety of plants, including members of the Myrtaceae, Asteraceae, and Rosaceae families. Despite feeding on fruits and seeds, Rosellas are not useful to the plants as seed-spreaders, because they crush and destroy the seeds in the process of eating them. Their diet often puts them at odds with farmers whose fruit and grain harvests can be damaged by the birds, which has resulted in large numbers of Rosellas being shot in the past. Rosellas will also eat many insects and their larvae, including termites, aphids, beetles, weevils, caterpillars, moths, and water boatmen.

Breeding

Adult on the left and juvenile on the right. The juvenile retains some green plumage.

Nesting sites are hollows greater than 1 metre (3 feet) deep in tree trunks, limbs, and stumps. These may be up to 30 metres (100 feet) above the ground. The nesting site is selected by the female. Once the site is selected, the pair will prepare it by lining it with wood debris made from the hollow itself by gnawing and shredding it with their beaks. They do not bring in material from outside the hollow. Only one pair will nest in a particular tree. A pair will guard their nest by perching near it at chattering at other Rosellas that approach. They will also guard a buffer zone of several trees radius around their nest, preventing other pairs from nesting in that area.

The breeding season of the Crimson Rosella lasts from September through to February, and varies depending on the rainfall of each year; it starts earlier and lasts longer during wet years. The laying period is on average during mid- to late October. Clutch size ranges from 3-8 eggs, which are laid asynchronously at an average interval of 2.1 days; the eggs are white and slightly shiny and measure 28 x 23 mm. The mean incubation period is 19.7 days, and ranges from 16–28 days. Only the mother incubates the eggs. The eggs hatch around mid December; on average 3.6 eggs successfully hatch. There is a bias towards female nestlings, as 41.8% of young are male. For the first six days, only the mother feeds the nestlings. After this time, both parents feed them. The young become independent in February, after which they spend a few more weeks with their parents before departing to become part of a flock of juveniles. Juveniles reach maturity (gain adult plumage) at 16 months of age.

Mutations

Next to the nominate bird which is mainly red coloured a few other colour mutations exist such as the blue, yellow, white and cinnamon mutations.

Threats

Crimson Rosellas may be eaten by cats or dogs, and have been found to make up a small part of the diet of the fox in some areas. Possums and currawongs are also believed to occasionally take eggs from the nest. Surprisingly, however, the Crimson Rosella is its own worst enemy. During the breeding season, it is common for females to fly to other nests and destroy the eggs. In fact, this is the most common cause for an egg failing to hatch. This behaviour is thought to be a function of competition for suitable nesting hollows, since a nest will be abandoned if all the eggs in it are destroyed, and a pair of Rosellas will tend to nest in the same area from year to year.

Source (edited): "http://en.wikipedia.org/wiki/Crimson_Rosella"

Eastern Ground Parrot

The **Eastern Ground Parrot** (*Pezoporus wallicus*) of Australia is one of only five ground-dwelling parrots in the world, the others being its closest relatives, the Western Ground Parrot (*Pezoporus flaviventris*), the extremely rare Night Parrot (*Pezoporus occidentalis*), the somewhat closely related Antipodes Parakeet (*Cyanoramphus unicolor*), and the unrelated highly endangered Kakapo (*Strigops habroptila*) from New Zealand.

The colouration of the three *Pezoporus* species and the Kakapo is similar – yellowish-green with darker barring, somewhat reminiscent of the head and back of the wild-type budgerigar. This is not an indication of a true relationship, however, but either adaptation to a particular lifestyle or a feature retained from ancestral parrots; probably the latter as barred plumage is found all over the family, from the tiny tiger parrots to female cockatiels.

When disturbed, ground parrots flies swiftly just above the ground before dropping back into the vegetation. The presence of the bird is often only revealed by its characteristic dusk and dawn call, a clear whistling sequence of notes which rise in pitch before fading. It is silent in flight.

Taxonomy

Traditionally, two subspecies are recognized within the Eastern Ground Parrot, but recent molecular studies show no genetic differentiation between the two east coast individuals and the individuals from Tasmania. Until recently, the Western Ground Parrot was also considered a subspecies (*Pezoporus wallicus flaviventris*) but is now considered a separate species (*Pezoporus flaviventris*).

The Eastern Ground Parrot (*Pezoporus wallicus wallicus*) occurs in fragmented populations near the coast in southern Queensland, New South Wales (NSW) and Victoria and is considered vulnerable on the schedules of the NSW Threatened Species Conservation Act. There are estimated to be 4000 breeding birds. It has become extinct in South Australia.

The Tasmanian Ground Parrot (*Pezoporus wallicus leachi*) is not considered threatened at state level and is most common in south west Tasmania.

Description

At Cooloolah NP, SE Queensland, Australia

Up to 30 cm long. Plumage grass green, each feather with black and yellow markings; narrow orange-red band to forehead; head, nape, upper back and breast green, each feather with black shaft marking; feathers of abdomen, thighs and under tail-coverts greenish-yellow with black barring; under wing-coverts green; primary coverts green; flight-feathers green with pale stripe across them; underside of flight-feathers with pale yellow wing-stripe; upperside of tail-feathers green with yellowish striped markings, underside brownish; outer tail-feathers yellow with brownish-black striping; bill greyish-brown to horn-colour; cere greyish-pink; narrow periophthalmic ring pale grey; iris whitish-yellow; longish feet greyish-brown; claws not so curved as other parrots.

Immatures as adults, but with slightly duller plumage; orange-red band to forehead absent; head, nape, upper back and breast green, each feather with distinct black shaft markings; tail shorter; iris brown.

Distribution

Extreme southeast of Queensland to southwest Australia (scattered in small groups); Tasmania and some off-shore islands.

Habitat

Marshy coastal plain without trees, reed beds with low bushes, restricted to button grass areas; species may depend on naturally occurring fires allowing new growth and renewed settlement by the Ground Parrot.

Status

Only found in certain localities; threatened in parts of its range by cultivation of large coastal areas, but also foxes, cats and fire; alleged to have strong scent and therefore easily disturbed by dogs.

Breeding

Breeding period from September to January; (one record in March); nest consisted of an excavation in soil 15 cm to 18 cm across and 2 cm (0.75 ins) to 5 cm deep; usually well hidden under small bush or tussock hanging over nest to provide a form of hollow; mostly lined with leaves, grass stalks, fern and small twigs; clutch 3 to 4 eggs; incubation probably 21 days; chicks well camouflaged with thick greyish-black down and protected against cold periods; young remain in nest for two weeks approaching parents for food; fed three times daily; leave nest after three weeks at least disturbance; roost after 25 days outside under tussocks; cannot however fly at this point; egg measures 28.1 x 22.2 mm.

Source (edited): "http://en.wikipedia.org/wiki/Eastern_Ground_Parrot"

Eastern Rosella

Eastern Rosella

The **Eastern Rosella** (*Platycercus eximius*) is a rosella native to southeast of the Australian continent and to Tasmania. It has been introduced to New Zealand where feral populations are found in the North Island (notably in the northern half of the island and in the Hutt Valley) and in the hills around Dunedin in the South Island.

Taxonomy

The Eastern Rosella was named by George Shaw in 1792. It is sometimes considered a subspecies of the Pale-headed Rosella (*P. adscitus*). The term White-cheeked Rosella has been used for a species or superspecies combining the Pale-headed and Eastern forms. Hybrids of the two taxa have been recorded where their ranges meet in northeastern New South Wales and southeastern Queensland.

Three subspecies of Eastern Rosella are recognised:
- *P. e. eximius*, Victoria and southern New South Wales. Black feathers on the back have green margins. Rump is pale green.
- *P. e. elecica*, northeast New South Wales and southeast Queensland. In the male the black feathers on the back have golden-yellow margins, and greenish-yellow in the female. The rump is bluish-green. This subspecies is also called the **Golden-mantled Rosella**, often abbreviated to GMR.
- *P. e. diemenensis*, eastern Tasmania. White cheek patches are larger and the red on the head is darker.

Description

Golden-mantled Rosella (*P. e. elecica*) at Woodland Park Zoo, USA. Feathers on the back of the male are edged with a golden-yellow colour.

The Eastern Rosella is 30 cm (12 in) long. It has a red head and white cheeks. The beak is white and the irises are brown. The upper breast is red and the lower breast is yellow fading to pale green over the abdomen. The feathers of the back and shoulders are black, and have yellowish or greenish margins giving rise to a scalloped appearance that varies slightly between the subspecies and the sexes. The wings and lateral tail feathers are bluish while the tail is dark green. The legs are grey. The female is similar to the male though duller in colouration and have an underwing stripe, which is not present in the adult male. Juveniles are duller than females and have an underwing stripe.

Distribution and habitat

The Eastern Rosella is found in lightly wooded country. It eats grass seeds and fruits. Breeding occurs in spring and early summer and up to seven white eggs are laid in tree hollows.

Breeding

Juvenile *P. e. diemenensis*

Chicks in nest

The breeding season is August to January, with one brood. The nesting site is usually a hollow over 1 m (3 ft) deep in a tree trunk anywhere up to 30 m (100 ft) above the ground. A clutch of generally five or six (although up to nine have been recorded) round, white and slightly shiny eggs, measuring 26 x 22 mm, is laid.

As pets

The Eastern Rosella is sometimes kept as a pet. These birds are desired for their beautifully coloured plumage. They are intelligent creatures, which can be trained to whistle a wide repertoire of tunes and may even learn to speak a few words or phrases. Rosellas can make good companion parrots; however, they require a great deal of attention and many toys to satisfy their need for social interaction and mental stimulation. These birds do not always adapt to life as a family pet and even hand-raised birds may never become fully domesticated. Generally, this species does not tolerate "petting" or "cuddling" and is apt to bite in response to this type of handling. Many people believe that Rosellas are best housed in large aviaries that enable them to fly freely with minimal human socialization. Despite these difficulties, many people enjoy the Eastern Rosella as a beautiful pet with a strong, feisty personality.

Source (edited): "http://en.wikipedia.org/wiki/Eastern_Rosella"

Golden-shouldered Parrot

The **Golden-shouldered Parrot** (*Psephotus chrysopterygius*) is a rare bird of southern Cape York Peninsula, in Queensland, Australia. A small attractive parrot related to the more common Red-rumped Parrot, it is considered to be a superspecies with the Hooded Parrot *(P. dissimilis)* of the Northern Territory and the apparently extinct Paradise Parrot of Queensland and New South Wales. It is 23–28 cm long and weighs 54–56 g.

Description
The Golden-shouldered Parrot is 23–28 cm long. The adult male is mainly blue and has a characteristic yellow over the shoulder area. It has a black cap and pale yellow frontal band. It has a pinkish lower belly, thighs and undertail-coverts. It has a Grey-brown lower back. Adult female are mainly dull greenish-yellow, and have a broad cream bar on the underside of the wings. Juveniles are similar to the adult female.

Habitat
The Golden-shouldered Parrot lives in open forest, where it feeds on small grass seeds, principally those of firegrass. An important habitat requirement is the provision of terrestrial termite mounds, which the bird uses for nesting in. This has led to the parrot also being known as the Antbed Parrot.

Breeding
The Golden-shouldered Parrot will build a nest in the taller termite mounds (up to 2 m high), and will dig a burrow into them when the mound has been softened by the rains. A long tunnel is dug down into the mound, and capped off by a nesting chamber. The clutch size is between 3–6 eggs, which are incubated for 20 days. The mound regulates the temperature of the nest in the chamber, so that the eggs can be left unattended while the parents feed.

Status
The Golden-shouldered Parrot is listed as endangered (CITES I). The species has a restricted range and suffers from a variety of threats, including predation by feral cats, tourist disturbance, feral pigs, and a change in burning regime in the grasslands upon whose seeds it depends. The wild population is around 3000 birds, with around 1500 kept in captivity in Australia.

Gallery

Male Golden-Shouldered Parrot in an aviary at the Queensland Museum. (photo 2004)

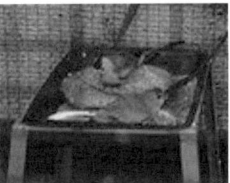

Male and female Golden-shouldered Parrots in an aviary at the Queensland Museum (photo 2004)

Male and female Golden-shouldered Parrots in an aviary at the Queensland Museum (photo 2004)

Source (edited): "http://en.wikipedia.org/wiki/Golden-shouldered_Parrot"

Green Rosella

The **Green Rosella** or **Tasmanian Rosella** (*Platycercus caledonicus*) is endemic to Tasmania and Bass Strait islands. At 37 cm (14.5 in) long it is the largest species of the *Rosella* genus. The male and female are generally similar in plumage, being predominantly black, green, and yellow in colour with a red band above the beak and blue cheeks; however, some females have red-orange colouration on the front of their necks. Its diet is composed of seeds, fruit, berries and flowers, as well as insects and insect larvae.

Taxonomy
The Green Rosella was described by the German naturalist Johann Friedrich Gmelin in 1788. The species specific epithet was derived from the mistaken belief the bird was collected from New Caledonia. Alternate common names include Tasmanian Rosella, Yellow-bellied or Yellow-breasted Parakeet, and Mountain Parrot.

Description

Male in Tasmania

Measuring 37 cm (14.5 in) in length, the adult Green Rosella has a yellow head and underparts with blue cheeks and red frontal band above the beak. The feathers of the back and wings are black with narrow green margins, the is rump yellow-olive, and the long tail is green with blue outer feathers. The wings are green and violet blue. The irises are dark brown and the bill is pale-grey. The legs are grey. The male and female have similar external appearances, except the female may have an orange-red hue in the feathers on the front of the neck, and the female has a smaller beak than the male. and Juvenile birds have an under-wing stripe, which is not present in the adults. Juveniles have dull yellow-green head and underparts and dull green upperparts.

Distribution and habitat

The Green Rosella is found across Tasmania and Bass Strait islands, and occurs in most habitats with some form of tree cover up to 1500 m ASL.

Feeding

Juvenile in Tasmania. It is greener than an adult

The Green Rosella is predominantly herbivorous, consuming seeds, berries, nuts and fruit, as well as flowers, but may also eat insect larvae and insects such as psyllids. They have also partaken of the berries of the common hawthorn (*Crataegus monogyna*), as well as *Coprosma* and *Cyathodes*, and even leaf buds of the Common Osier (*Salix viminalis*). The seeds of the Silver Wattle (*Acacia dealbata*) are also eaten.

Breeding

The breeding season is October to January, with one brood. The nesting site is usually a hollow over 1 m (3 ft) deep in a tree trunk anywhere up to 30 m (100 ft) above the ground. A clutch of four or five white and slightly shiny eggs, measuring 30 x 24 mm, is laid. The nestlings leave the nest around five weeks after hatching and remain with their parents for another month.

Aviculture

The Green Rosella is reported to be hardier and easier to keep in captivity than other rosellas.
Source (edited): "http://en.wikipedia.org/wiki/Green_Rosella"

Mulga Parrot

The **Mulga Parrot** (*Psephotus varius*), also known as the **Many-coloured Parrot**, is endemic in arid scrublands and lightly timbered grasslands in the interior of southern Australia.

Taxonomy

The Mulga Parrot was given its current scientific name of *Psephotus varius* by American zoologist Austin Hobart Clark in 1910, after its name *Psephotus multicolor* was ruled invalid as the original combination (*Psittacus multicolor*) had been used for another species. It is one of five species in the *Psephotus*.

Common names include the Mulga Parrot, Many-coloured Parrot, and Varied Parrot.

Description

Male on the left and female on the right in Currawinya National Park in south west Queensland

The male Mulga Parrot is multicolored from which the common name Many-coloured Parrot of this species is derived. It is a bright green overall, with a bluish tinge on the neck and above the eye, and paler on the breast. The rump is light green. The forehead is yellow and there is a red patch on the back of the head. The lower belly and thighs are yellowish marked with orange-red and the wings greenish apart from the yellow median wing coverts and blue outer webs of primaries. The long tail is an assortment of colours: the two long central feathers are dark blue tinged with green, the outer feathers are blue shading to white and there is some red on the upper tail coverts. Its bill is a blue-grey edged with black, and iris is brown. The female is duller overall, with an olive-brown head and chest, duller yellow forehead and red patch on the back of the head, and pale green belly, and more brown-grey bill. It has a red shoulder.

Distribution and habitat

The species ranges across the dryer interior of the Australian continent, from Western New South Wales from Collarenabri, West Wyalong and Griffith westwards through the northwestern tip of Victoria and across South Australia and into the dryer central regions of Western Australia west to the Wheatbelt and north to the Pilbara. The Mulga Parrot is generally encountered in pairs in arid grassland and mulga scrubland.

Breeding

Breeding season is anywhere from July to December or after rainfall, with one or occasionally two broods raised depending on rainfall. A hollow in a tree is utilised for nesting, and a clutch of four to six white eggs measuring 22 x 18 mm is laid there.

Source (edited): "http://en.wikipedia.org/wiki/Mulga_Parrot"

Night Parrot

The **Night Parrot** (*Pezoporus occidentalis*) is a small broad-tailed parrot endemic to the continent of Australia. The species was originally placed within its own genus (*Geopsittacus*), but most authors now prefer to place it within the genus *Pezoporus* together with the two ground parrots.

No known sightings of the bird were made between 1912 and 1979, leading to speculation that it was extinct. Sightings since 1979 have been extremely rare and the bird's population size is unknown.

Description

A relatively small parrot, the species' colour is predominantly a yellowish green, mottled with dark brown, blacks and yellows. It is distinguished from the two superficially similar ground parrot species by its shorter tail and different range and habitat. Predominantly terrestrial, taking to the air only when panicked or in search of water, the Night Parrot has furtive, nocturnal habits and—even when it was abundant—was apparently a highly secretive species. Its natural habitat appears to be the spinifex grass which still dominates much of the dry, dusty Australian interior; other early reports also indicate that it never strayed far from water.

Conservation status

The population size of this species is not known. Estimates range from extinct to not threatened at all. It is currently listed on the IUCN Red List as Critically Endangered.

There have been only a few reliable records of the bird since the 1880s, with the last authenticated report dating from 2006, when rangers found a dead specimen which had flown into a barbed wire fence in the Diamantina National Park in south western Queensland. Prior to this, the last reliable sighting was of three individuals in 2005 near Minga Well, in the Pilbara region of Western Australia. Reliable sightings were made in 1990 when a roadkill specimen was discovered by scientists returning from an expedition in a remote part of Queensland and 1979 when Ornithologist Shane A. Parker from the South Australian Museum spotted an apparent flock of the birds in the far north of South Australia.

Ornithologists continue to patrol the outback for signs that the species still thrives, even checking the old nests of other birds, such as the Zebra Finch, for fragments of Night Parrot feathers. The Night Parrot remains one of the most elusive and mysterious birds in the world of ornithology.

Sightings at Minga Well

The approval of the A$2billion Cloud Break mine project through the then-Minister for the Environment, Ian Campbell, was criticised because of a number of endangered species in the area of the future mine, among them the Night Parrot. In order to gain EPA approval, the mine had to implement a management plan to ensure that mining activities would not have a negative effect on the species survival in the area.

The occurrence of the Night Parrot in the future mining area, at Minga Well on 12 April 2005, was discovered during a 2005 survey commissioned by FMG, which was carried out by two contract biologists who sighted a small group of the birds. Unconfirmed sightings of the bird had been made previously in a near-by area in 2004.

The sighting, at dusk, was by biologists Dr Robert Davis and Mr Brendan Metcalf, who were not able to obtain a photograph of the three birds they saw, but are confident that they spotted three Night Parrots. The detailed descriptions of their sighting were accepted by the Birds Australia Rarities Committee (BARC) making it the only accepted Night Parrot sighting in modern times. Based on this acceptance by scientific peers, a paper describing the sighting was published in the Australian ornithological journal, Emu in 2008. The two biologists carried out further searches at Minga Well and Moojari Well the following five nights after the sighting, but were unable to spot the birds again. A follow up survey of the Fortescue Marsh area in May 2005 was unsuccessful in finding any conclusive evidence of the species.

List of sightings

- April 2005, Pilbara region of Western Australia and near the Fortescue Marshes
- September 2006, dead female, Diamantina National Park.

Source (edited): "http://en.wikipedia.org/wiki/Night_Parrot"

Northern Rosella

The **Northern Rosella** (*Platycercus venustus*), also known as **Brown's Parakeet** or **Smutty Rosella**, is found in Australia's Top End. It is unusually coloured for a rosella, with a dark crown and white cheeks similar to its relatives the Pale-headed Rosella and the Eastern Rosella.

At 28 cm long it is smaller than all bar the Western Rosella. The forehead, crown and nape are black in colour with white-on-blue cheek-patches. The back and wing feathers are blackish with yellow borders, while the feathers of the belly, chest and rump are pale yellow with black borders giving rise to a scalloped appearance. The long tail is bluish green. The beak is pale grey and the iris dark. Immature plumage is similar to adult but duller.

The Northern Rosella is found from the Gulf of Carpentaria, through Arnhem Land to the Kimberleys in open savannah country.

It is not a gregarious bird, found solitarily or in pairs. Nesting occurs in tree hollows in winter, with two to four eggs laid.

The Northern Rosella was first described by German naturalist Heinrich Kuhl. The specific epithet is derived from the Latin *venustus* "charming, lovely or graceful". A subspecies, var. *hilli*, was described by Mathews in 1910, however is not felt to be valid.

In captivity, they are said to continue with their early mating habit, which is not a problem in Australia but more so in other countries.

Source (edited): "http://en.wikipedia.org/wiki/Northern_Rosella"

Orange-bellied Parrot

The **Orange-bellied Parrot** (*Neophema chrysogaster*) is a small broad-tailed parrot endemic to southern Australia, and one of only two species of parrot which migrate. The adult male is distinguished by its bright grass-green upperparts, yellow underparts and orange belly patch. The adult female and juvenile are duller green in colour. All birds have a blue frontal band and blue outer wing feathers. The diet consists of seeds and berries of small coastal grasses and shrubs.

The Orange-bellied Parrot breeds in Tasmania and winters in coastal grasslands on southern mainland Australia. With a population in the wild of fewer than 35 to 50 wild birds, it is regarded as a critically endangered species. Recent alarming declines in the wild population of Orange-bellied parrots has prompted the Australian Government to decide in April 2010 that it would capture up to 20 of the remaining wild population to further improve the genetic diversity of the species' captive breeding program as an "insurance" against extinction.

Taxonomy and naming

The Orange-bellied Parrot was first described by ornithologist John Latham in 1790. He gave it the specific name, *chrysogaster*, Ancient Greek for 'golden belly'. No subspecies are recognised. It is one of six species of grass parrot in the genus *Neophema*. It has previously been known as the Orange-breasted Parrot - a name given to the Orange-bellied Parrot in 1926 by the Royal Australasian Ornithologists Union or RAOU (now known as Birds Australia) when the word 'belly' was considered inelegant.

Description

The Orange-bellied Parrot is a small parrot around 20 cm (8 in) long; the adult male has bright green upperparts, and yellow below with a prominent, two-toned blue frontal band, a green-blue uppertail with yellow sides, and an orange patch on its belly. The under wing-coverts and flight feathers are dark blue, with paler blue median wing-coverts. Its iris is dark brown and beak and feet greyish. The adult female is a duller green with a paler blue frontal band. The juvenile is a duller green colour.

The Orange-bellied parrot utters soft tinkling notes, as well as a distinctive rapidly repeated chittering alarm call unlike that of other members of the genus. The alarm call is a quickly repeated tzeet.

Distribution and habitat

Orange-bellied Parrots only breed in South West Tasmania, where they nest in eucalypts bordering on button grass moors. The entire population migrates over Bass Strait to spend the winter on the coast of south-eastern Australia. These few sites contain their favoured salt marsh habitat, and includes sites in or close to Port Phillip such as Werribee Sewage Farm, the Spit Nature Conservation Reserve, the shores of Swan Bay, Swan Island, Lake Connewarre State Wildlife Reserve, Lake Victoria and Mud Islands, as well as French Island in Western Port.

Behaviour

The Orange-bellied Parrot is found in pairs or small flocks, and generally remain on the ground or in low foliage searching for food. Their diet consists of seeds of species such as the grass *Poa biliarderi*, saltbush (*Atriplex cinerea*), *Suaeda australis* and sea heath (*Frankenia pauciflora*), as well as berries, such as those of *Coprosma*. They have also been reported eating kelp.

Reproduction

Breeding season is October to January with one brood raised. The nest is a hollow in a tree, less than 5 m (16 ft) above the ground. Four or five white eggs are laid measuring 20 mm x 23 mm.

Conservation status

This species has a very small population and is on the verge of extinction in the wild. It is listed on the IUCN Red List as Critically Endangered. The current wild population is estimated at under 50 individuals, with a further 160 birds in captive breeding programs. Recent modelling suggests that on current trends the species will become extinct in the wild within five years.

There are now estimated to be about 35 individuals in the wild and only five have made the winter migration to the mainland so far in 2011. In May 2011, 10 individuals were captured and transferred by aircraft from Tasmania to Healesville Sanctuary near Melbourne in a last ditch effort to save the species from extinction. It is hoped that the new additions from the wild will improve the genetic diversity of the 80 birds at Healesville Sanctuary, which are all bred from three pairs. Captive populations in Hobart and Adelaide are also important to the aim of releasing captive bred birds back to the wild.

International
It is listed as critically endangered on the IUCN Red List.

Australia
- In 2007, its status was upgraded from endangered to critically endangered on the Commonwealth *Environment Protection and Biodiversity Conservation Act 1999*.
- The 2000 Action Plan for Australian Birds lists it as critically endangered (Garnett and Crowley 2000).
- In a report on threatened and extinct birds in Australia in 1992, it was listed as endangered (Garnett 1992).
- In a report on threatened birds in Australia in 1990, it was listed as endangered (Brouwer and Garnett 1990).

State Level
The Orange-bellied Parrot has been recorded from four states within Australia; Tasmania, Victoria, New South Wales and South Australia. Its conservation status varies from state to state within Australia. For example:
- The Orange-bellied Parrot is listed as **threatened** on the Victorian Flora and Fauna Guarantee Act (1988). Under this Act, an *Action Statement* for the recovery and future management of this species has been prepared.
- On the 2007 advisory list of threatened vertebrate fauna in Victoria, the Orange-bellied Parrot is listed as **critically endangered**.

Threats
The 2000 Action Plan for Australian Birds identifies the following potential threats to the Orange-bellied Parrot:
- Fragmentation and degradation of over-wintering habitat
- Competition with introduced seed-eaters
- Abandonment of former breeding habitat due to altered fire regime and competition for hollows (with the introduced Common Starling)
- Random events due to the small size of the population
- Disorientation from brightly lit fishing boats (during the migrations across Bass Strait)
- Introduced predators
- Disease (such as Psittacine Circoviral Disease)

Other identified potential threats include:
- Lack of safety in numbers for a small bird attractive to avian predators (Brouwer and Garnett 1990)
- Historically was trapped for aviculture (Garnett 1992)
- A stomach virus is threatening a breeding program for the critically endangered orange-bellied parrot.

Conflict with development
The Woolnorth windfarm on Tasmania's North-West coast is operating with a license to kill up to six Orange-bellied Parrots every two years. In 2001, then Australian federal environment minister Robert Hill approved the wind farm, along the main migratory flight path for the parrot, with several conditions to protect migrating birds. To date no Orange-bellied Parrots have been found to collide with the turbines.

The Orange-bellied Parrot earned the wrath of Victorian premier Jeff Kennett in the 1990s. A proposed relocation of the Coode Island Chemical storage facility to a location near Point Wilson, Victoria was jeopardised by the potential impacts upon Orange-bellied Parrot habitat. Mr Kennett famously described this species as a 'trumped-up corella'. This moniker was later adopted as the title for the Orange-bellied Parrot Recovery Teams newsletter.

In 2006, the potential threats to the Orange-bellied Parrot were cited as the key reason for Commonwealth Minister rejecting the proposal to build the Bald Hills Wind Farm in eastern Victoria. This decision was later reversed, and the company was provided with approval to proceed (under certain conditions). The intense media scrutiny at this time placed the Orange-bellied Parrot temporarily into the spotlight. In the subsequent months, additional funding was provided for the parrots recovery, and its status under the Commonwealth Environment Protection and Biodiversity Conservation Act 1999 was raised from *endangered* to *critically endangered*.

Source (edited): "http://en.wikipedia.org/wiki/Orange-bellied_Parrot"

Pale-headed Rosella

The **Pale-headed Rosella** (*Platycercus adscitus*), is a broad-tailed parrot of the genus *Platycercus* native to northeastern Australia. It is a moderate-size parrot with a pale yellow head, predominantly white cheeks, scalloped black and gold back and pale blue underparts. Two subspecies are recognised, although some authorities consider it to be conspecific with the Eastern Rosella of southeastern Australia.

Found in open woodland, it feeds on seeds and fruit. As with other rosellas, the Pale-headed Rosella nests in hollows of large trees. It readily adapts to aviculture and is sold as a cagebird.

Taxonomy
The Pale-headed Rosella was first described by English ornithologist John Latham in 1790. There are two subspecies, the better known *palliceps* (eastern Queensland), known as the Blue-cheeked Rosella, and *adscitus* (Cape York Peninsula). Its closest relative is the Eastern Rosella, which replaces it in southeastern Australia. Hybrids of the two taxa have been recorded where their ranges meet in northeastern New South Wales and southeastern

Queensland. Some consider the two conspecific; this would add another three subspecies.

Other common names occasionally seen include Mealy Rosella, Moreton Bay Rosella, Blue Rosella, and Blue-cheeked Rosella for the northern subspecies. The term White-cheeked Rosella has been used for a species or superspecies combining the Pale-headed and Eastern forms.

Description

In Atherton Tablelands, Australia

The Pale-headed Rosella is 33 cm (13 in) long, which includes the 15 cm length of its tail. Its underparts are pale blue, and upper breast and head are pale cream-yellow, the tail which is blue-black and green and the vent which is blood red. The feathers of the nape, scapulars and back are black edged with bright yellow, giving rise to a scalloped appearance. In these margins of the northern race, the yellow is paler with a pale blue tinge. The cheeks are wholly white in the southern subspecies, and partly flushed with blue in the lower-parts in the northern subspecies. The bill is pale blue-white and the legs dark grey. The eyes are yellow-brown. The sexes are similar in appearance, although the female is slightly smaller and duller.

Distribution and habitat

The nominate subspecies *adscitus* is found from the Cape York Peninsula south through to Cardwell in central-northern Queensland. There is a broad range of intermediate forms, while the southern subspecies *palliceps* extends from Townsville and points inland south into northeastern New South Wales to the vicinity of the Clarence River. It is common throughout its range. Its preferred habitat is open forest, but has adapted well to human modification of the rural landscape and may even become a pest to orchards and cereal crops. Watering troughs help the species in the dryer western limits of its range.

It was also introduced to Hawaii in 1877, but had died out there by the late 1920s.

Feeding

In Dayboro, SE Queensland

It eats grass and tree seeds and fruits, including River Red-gum (*Eucalyptus camaldulensis*), River Sheoak (*Casuarina cunninghamiana*), Snow-in-summer (*Melaleuca linariifolia*) and other melaleucas, and Rough Cockleburr (*Xanthium strumarium*). Birds are partial to the introduced Scotch Thistle (*Onopordum acanthium*).

Breeding

The breeding season varies according to region, with southern birds nesting from September to December and northern ones later from February to June. One brood is laid. The nesting site is usually a hollow over 1 m (3 ft) deep in a tree trunk anywhere up to 30 m (100 ft) above the ground. A clutch of five or six (although up to nine have been recorded) round, white and slightly shiny eggs, measuring 26 x 22 mm, is laid.

Aviculture

The species is relatively hardy and easy to keep in cultivation. It can be aggressive and so is recommended to be segregated from other birds in captivity.
Source (edited): "http://en.wikipedia.org/wiki/Pale-headed_Rosella"

Paradise Parrot

The **Paradise Parrot** (*Psephotus pulcherrimus*) was an unusually colourful medium-sized parrot native to the grassy woodlands of the Queensland - New South Wales border area of northeastern Australia. Once moderately common within its fairly restricted range, the last live bird was seen in 1927. Extensive and sustained searches in the years since then have failed to produce any reliable evidence of it, and it is unknown if it is extinct or not.

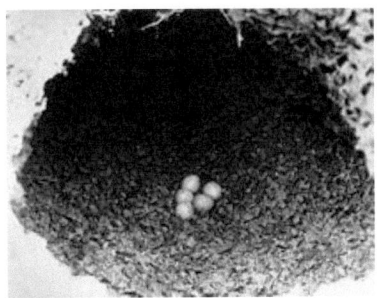
Nest, 1922

Two specimens by a nest, 1922

Painting from 1884

of its time on the ground.

The reasons for the sudden decline of the Paradise Parrot remain speculative. Possibilities include overgrazing, land clearing, changed fire regimes, hunting by bird collectors, and predation by introduced mammals like cats. It became rare towards the end of the 19th century and was thought extinct by 1915. A series of searches turned up a few more individuals over the next decade, but the last confirmed sighting was on 14 September 1927.

Source (edited): "http://en.wikipedia.org/wiki/Paradise_Parrot"

Paradise Parrots lived in pairs or small family groups, making their nests in hollowed-out termite mounds and similar places, often at or near ground level, and feeding, so far as is known, almost exclusively on grass seeds.

The plumage was extraordinarily colorful, even by parrot standards, a mixture of turquoise, aqua, scarlet, black and brown, and the tail almost the same length as the body—something difficult to understand in a bird that, although a rapid, undulating flyer, spent almost all

Pezoporus

The genus **Pezoporus** contains three Australian species: the Night Parrot (*Pezoporus occidentalis*) and the cryptic ground parrots, the Eastern Ground Parrot (*Pezoporus wallicus*) and the Western Ground Parrot (*Pezoporus flaviventris*). The night parrot was previously separated in a distinct genus, *Geopsittacus*. The genus is considered part of the tribe Platycercini or, if this is considered a subfamily, the monotypic tribe **Pezoporini**. The phylogenetic position of the genus **Pezoporus** within the parrot family remains unclear.

- Genus **Pezoporus**

Source (edited): "http://en.wikipedia.org/wiki/Pezoporus"

Psephotus

The genus **Psephotus** has five species of parakeets from Australia. All species show considerable sexual dimorphism.

Systematics

Subgenus *Psephotus*:
- Red-rumped Parrot, *Psephotus haematonotus*
- Mulga Parrot, *Psephotus varius*

Subgenus *Psephotellus*:
- Hooded Parrot, *Psephotus dissimilis*
- Golden-shouldered Parrot, *Psephotus chrysopterygius*
- Paradise Parrot, *Psephotus pulcherrimus*

Species photographs

Red-rumped Parrot

Mulga Parrot

Hooded Parrot (female)

Golden-shouldered Parrot

Source (edited): "http://en.wikipedia.org/wiki/Psephotus"

Red-capped Parrot

The **Red-capped Parrot** (*Purpureicephalus spurius*), also called the **Pileated Parakeet** (leading to easy confusion with the South American *Pionopsitta pileata*), and **King Parrot** locally in Western Australia, is an Australian species of broad-tailed parrot related to the Rosellas.

First described by German naturalist Heinrich Kuhl in 1820, from a collection in Albany, Western Australia, the Red-capped Parrot was placed in the monotypic genus *Purpureicephalus* by Charles Lucien Bonaparte in 1854. The generic name is an amalgam of the Latin *purpureus* "purple", and the Ancient Greek *kephalos* "head". The specific epithet *spurius* is the Latin adjective meaning "illegitimate", and refers to the very different adult and immature plumages (hence appearing unrelated). Besides Red-capped Parrot, vernacular names include Pileated Parrot, Western King Parrot, Purple-crowned Parrot, Grey Parrot or Hookbill.

Measuring 34–38 cm (14–15 in) in length and weighing 105–125 g, the adult Red-capped Parrot is a distinctive and easily recognised medium-sized parrot. The adult male has a crimson crown, grey-brown lores, and green-yellow cheeks and a narrow long upper mandible. The upperparts are dark green, the rump yellow-green, the tail green with dark blue tip. The underparts are purplish-blue and the flanks green and red. The female is similar but duller overall, and the juvenile has a dark green crown, reddish frontal band, and red-brown underparts.

The species occurs from the Moore River southwards in southwestern Australia. Its natural habitat is Marri (*Corymbia calophylla*), but has adpated to farmland, orchards and suburban landscapes in Perth.

Marri seeds are the preferred diet, but birds also extract seeds from Karri (*Eucalyptus marginata*), woody pear (*Xylomelum*), *Grevillea*, *Hakea*, and Sheoak (*Casuarina*), as well as insects such as psyllids, and even orchard fruit such as apples and pears.

The breeding season is August to December, the nest is a tree hollow, and a clutch of five white [[bird egg|egg\\s is laid.

Source (edited): "http://en.wikipedia.org/wiki/Red-capped_Parrot"

Red-rumped Parrot

The **Red-rumped Parrot** (*Psephotus haematonotus*), also known as the **Red-backed Parrot** or **Grass Parrot**, is a common bird of south-eastern Australia, particularly in the Murray-Darling Basin.

Description

Red-rumped Parrots are slim, elegant, moderate-sized parrots approximately 28 cm (11 in) in length. The male's plumage is a bright emerald-green with yellow underparts, a brick-red rump and blue highlights on the wings and upper back. The female's plumage is less vibrant, with pale olive underparts, dull green wings and back and blue-black wingtips. The characteristic red rump is only found in the male.

Behavior

Female (in foreground) and male at Eastern Creek, New South Wales, Australia

Red-rumped Parrots can be found in pairs or flocks in open country with access to water. They avoid the coast and the wetter, more heavily wooded areas. Clearing of large tracts of forest and the provision of water for stock has probably extended their range. They are often seen in suburban parks and gardens. Their green plumage provides such a good camouflage in ankle length grasses that they can hide quite effectively until the viewer is only 10-20 metres away.

They spend a great deal of time feeding on the ground, and often call to one another with an attractive *chee chillip chee chillip*.

Breeding

A pair in suburban Sydney, Australia

Like many parrots, Red-rumped Parrots nest in tree hollows or similar places, including fenceposts and stumps. They lay 4-6 white eggs, Breeding usually takes place in spring (August to January), however, in the dryer inland areas, breeding can occur at any time of year in response to rainfall.

Aviculture

Red rumps are bred easily in captivity if provided with necessary flight space and a large nesting box. Breeders usually use peat and wood shavings as bedding for the nests , birds like to arrange the beds to their likings. As soon as mating has occurred the hen will deposit 4 to 7 eggs which she will brood for about 20 days. Red rump hens will not go out of the nest box whilst on eggs and not even human checking will make them leave their eggs alone. The eggs will hatch around 30 days after and take care to remove the chicks as soon as they are fledged or else the cock may attack his own offspring. One-year-old birds are already able to breed. Incubation from the second egg onwards. The brooding hen is fed by her partner outside the nest.

Lifespan

If properly cared for these birds will live up to 15–20 years.
Source (edited): "http://en.wikipedia.org/wiki/Red-rumped_Parrot"

Rock Parrot

The **Rock Parrot** (*Neophema petrophila*), also known as the **Rock Elegant**, is a parrot which is endemic to coastal South Australia, southern Western Australia, and that continent's offshore islands, including Rottnest Island. It is a small, predominantly olive-green parrot. Grass seeds form the bulk of its diet.

Taxonomy

The Rock Parrot was described by ornithologist John Gould in 1841, its specific name *petrophila* derived from the Greek *petros*/πετρος 'rock' and *philos*/φιλος 'loving'.

Description

The Rock Parrot is 22 cm (9 in) long and predominantly olive-brown in colour with a dark blue frontal band line above with lighter blue. The lores and parts of the cheek are pale blue, this is less extensive in females. The breast is olive-grey, and duller in females, while abdomen and vent are yellow. The wings are predominantly olive with outer flight feathers blue. The yellow-edged tail has shades of olive and blue. The bill and legs are grey and the eyes dark brown. Juveniles are duller and lack the frontal bands.

Distribution and habitat

Rocky islands and coastal dune areas are the preferred habitats for this species, which is found from Robe, South Australia westwards across coastal South and Western Australia to Shark Bay.

Behaviour

Rock Parrots eat seeds of grasses, shrubs and succulent plants, such as *Carpobrotus* species, in coastal habitats. They can be approached easily while feeding.
Source (edited): "http://en.wikipedia.org/wiki/Rock_Parrot"

Rosella

A **rosella** is one of five to eight species of colorful Australian parrots in the genus **Platycercus**. *Platycercus* means "broad-tailed" or "flat-tailed", reflecting a feature common to the rosellas and other members of the broad-tailed parrot tribe. Their diet is mainly seeds and fruit.

Etymology

Early European settlers encountered the Eastern Rosella at Rose Hill, New South Wales, now Parramatta, and so they called it the Rosehill Parakeet, which became, "Rosehiller", and eventually "Rosella".

Description

Ranging in size from 26–37 cm (10–14.5 in), rosellas are medium-sized parrots with long tails. The feathers on their backs show an obvious scalloping appearance with colouring that differs between the species. All species have distinctive cheek patches. Sexual dimorphism is absent or slight - males and females generally have similar plumage, apart from the Western Rosella. The juveniles of the blue-cheeked species, and Western Rosella, all have a distinctive green-based plumage, while immature plumage of the white-cheeked species is merely a duller version of the adults.

Distribution and habitat

Rosellas are native to Australia and nearby islands, where they inhabit forests, woodlands, farmlands, and suburban parks and gardens. They are confined to the coastal mountains and plains and are absent from the outback. Introduced populations have also established themselves in New Zealand (notably in the North Island and in north Dunedin) and on Norfolk Island.

Behaviour and ecology

Rosellas feed predominantly on seeds and fruit, with food held in the foot. They enjoy bathing in puddles of water in the wild and in captivity. Rosellas scratch their heads with the foot behind the wing.

Mutual preening is not exhibited by the genus, and the courtship display is simple; the male waves his tail sideways, and engages in some head bobbing, and the female reciprocates.

Like most parrots, they are cavity nesters, generally nesting high in older large trees in forested areas. They generally have a clutch size of several eggs which are incubated for around 21 days by the female alone. The male feeds the female through this time and for some time after incubation concludes. Quickly covered in a white down, chicks take around five weeks to fledge.

Aviculture

The more colourful rosella species are popular as pet parrots and also as aviary birds. They can live for longer than 20 years, and they are relatively easy to breed. All have a reputation for being aggressive in captivity, and are hence recommended be kept separate from other caged birds. Their diet in aviculture includes seeds, fruit such as apple, pear, and grapes, and vegetable matter such as lettuce, grass, and silver beet.

Taxonomy

Green Rosella in Tasmania. It is the largest rosella at 37 cm (14.5 in) long

The genus was described by naturalist Nicholas Aylward Vigors in 1825; the name *Platycercus* derived from the Ancient Greek "broad-" or "flat-tailed". The relationships with other parrots have been unclear, with the Australian Ringneck cited as a closest relative by some, and the genus *Psephotus* by others; the plumage of the Western Rosella seen as a link to the latter genus.

There are, broadly speaking, three groups of rosella species. They are the blue cheeked species which includes *elegans* and *caledonicus*, the white cheeked species, *eximius*, *adscitus* and *venustus* and the yellow cheeked species, *icterotis*. The observed difference in plumage has been reinforced by molecular studies which place the *icterotis* as a basal offshoot.

There are six species and several subspecies:

Platycercus, Vigors 1825

- *Platycercus caledonicus*, (Gmelin 1788)
  - *Platycercus caledonicus brownii*, (Kuhl 1820)
  - *Platycercus caledonicus caledonicus*, (Gmelin 1788)
- *Platycercus elegans*, (Gmelin 1788)
  - *Platycercus elegans elegans*, (Gmelin 1788)
  - *Platycercus elegans flaveolus*, Gould 1837
  - *Platycercus elegans fleurieuensis*, Ashby 1917
  - *Platycercus elegans melanopterus*, North 1906
  - *Platycercus elegans nigrescens*, Ramsay, EP 1888
  - *Platycercus elegans subadelaidae*, Mathews 1912
- *Platycercus venustus*, (Kuhl 1820)
  - *Platycercus venustus hilli*, Mathews 1910
  - *Platycercus venustus venustus*, (Kuhl 1820)
- *Platycercus adscitus*, (Latham 1790)
  - *Platycercus adscitus adscitus*, (Latham 1790)
  - *Platycercus adscitus palliceps*, Lear 1832
- *Platycercus eximius*, (Shaw 1792)
  - *Platycercus eximius diemenensis*, North 1911
  - *Platycercus eximius elecica*, Schodde & Short 1989
  - *Platycercus eximius eximius*, (Shaw 1792)
- *Platycercus icterotis*, (Temminck & Kuhl 1820)
  - *Platycercus icterotis icterotis*, (Temminck & Kuhl 1820)
  - *Platycercus icterotis xanthogenys*, Salvadori 1891

Source (edited): "http://en.wikipedia.org/wiki/Rosella"

Scarlet-chested Parrot

The **Scarlet-chested Parrot** (*Neophema splendida*), known alternately as **Scarlet-breasted parrot**, **Orange-throated parrot** or **Splendid parrot**, is a parrot endemic to central South Australia and inland southern Western Australia. The species is sexually dimorphic; the male has a bright blue face and scarlet chest and yellow underparts, amid overall green plumage, while the female is similar but lacks the red chest. These nomadic parakeets move readily from the Great Victoria Desert region into neighbouring areas. These interruptions are triggered by a search for more favourable conditions. They can survive quite well without access to drinking water, however, as succulent plants help meet much of their fluid requirement. They feed mainly on grass seeds and are most commonly sighted in spinifex.

Taxonomy

The Scarlet-chested Parrot was originally named by the renowned ornithologist and artist John Gould in 1841 as *Euphema splendida*, before it was given its current binomial name in 1891 by moving into the new genus *Neophema*. Its specific name *splendida* is the Latin adjective "splendid". No subspecies are recognised. It is one of six species of grass parrot in the genus *Neophema*, and is most closely related to the Turquoise Parrot. Common names include *Scarlet-chested Parrot*, *Orange-throated Parrot*, *Splendid Parrot*, *Scarlet-breasted Parrot*, and *Scarlet-chested Parakeet* in aviculture.

Description

Measuring 19–21 cm (8 in) in length, this small brightly coloured parrot is sexually dimorphic. The male has a scarlet chest, a cobalt blue face, and bright green upperparts. The lower breast and underparts are yellow, and the wing coverts are pale blue. The tail is green, the eyes are brown and the bill is blackish, and legs are brown-grey. The female likewise has a blue face, although the coloration is less extensive, green upperparts and green breast, with yellow underparts. Immature birds are duller versions of their respective adult forms. Males begin to get red plumage on their chest from around two or three months of age, though do not complete their red chest until fifteen to eighteen months old.

The female resembles the female Turquoise Parrot (*N. pulchella*) of eastern Australia, but can be distinguished by the blue lores and paler blue wing patch.

The call is a soft twittering, quieter than other members of the genus *Neophema*.

The Scarlet-chested Parrot is sparsely scattered across the dryer southern parts of the Australian continent, from Pingelly, Corrigin and Laverton in Western Australia east across South Australia and into the southern Northern Territory and into far western New South Wales. It has been classified as *vulnerable* in New South Wales, the dangers highlighted include the harvesting of trees that are potential and actual nesting sites, as larger trees are necessary for suitable hollows, possible trapping for the pet trade, and grazing by stock and feral animals. They inhabit dry *Eucalyptus* and *Acacia* scrubland and grassland, including *Atriplex* and *Triodia*. True estimates of rarity or abundance are difficult to determine; although the bird is brightly coloured, it is secretive and easily overlooked.

Feeding

Seeds of grasses make up the diet, and they are thought to utilise succulent plants such as *Calandrinia* to meet much of their fluid requirement.

Breeding

Breeding season is from August to October or after rainfall, with one or occasionally two broods raised depending on rainfall. A hollow in a small tree, often a mulga or eucalypt, is utilised for nesting, and a clutch of four to six round white eggs measuring 23×19 mm is laid there.

Aviculture

Adult male at Cincinnati zoo, USA

The Scarlet-chested Parrot is becoming more common in captivity, and is one of the more popular species of the genus *Neophema* in captivity both in Australia and overseas. Their quiet temperament and small size increase their appeal as aviary birds. Many mutations are seen, including the red-fronted, par blue, sea green (Sydney Blue), white fronted blue (Recessive), cinnamon (sex-linked), and more rarely lutino and fallow. Although the species has more mutations than any other member of the genus, they tend to be frail healthwise and short-lived. Scarlet-chested Parrots are also vulnerable to *Candida* infections in aviculture.

Source (edited): "http://en.wikipedia.org/wiki/Scarlet-chested_Parrot"

Swift Parrot

Captive

The **Swift Parrot** (*Lathamus discolor*) breeds in Tasmania and migrates north to south eastern Australia from Griffith-Warialda in New South Wales and west to Adelaide in the winter. It is related to the rosellas, with the feeding habits of a lorikeet. It is the only member in the genus ***Lathamus***.

The Swift Parrot is endangered with only about 1000 pairs remaining in the wild, and its population is declining.

Description
The Swift Parrot is about 25 cm (10 in) long and has long pointed wings and long tapering tail feathers. It is mainly green with bluish crown and red on the face above and below the beak. The adult female is slightly duller, and the juvenile has a dark brown iris and a pale orange bill.

Breeding and social habits
The species breeds in Tasmania from September to December. It nests in tree hollows about 6–20 metres from ground level and usually with other breeding pairs. Eggs are white with 3–5 per clutch. Voice is of high pitched tinking chattering, piping pee-pit, pee-pit.

Migration
The Swift Parrot migrates across the Bass Strait between Tasmania and the mainland of Australia. They arrive in Tasmania during September and return to south-eastern Australia during March and April. They can be found as far north as south-eastern Queensland and as far west as Adelaide although recent sightings have been restricted to the Eastern part of the state.

Mudgereeba, SE Queensland, Australia

Habitat
Usually inhabiting: forests, woodlands, agricultural land and plantations, and also in urban areas.

Diet
Seeds and grains, green vegetation, fruit, nectar and pollen, insects and larvae.

Conservation status
It is thought that only 1000 pairs remain in the wild. Habitat destruction and loss of old trees with nesting hollows is the critical factor in its decline.

Australia
Swift Parrots are listed as endangered on the Australian Environment Protection and Biodiversity Conservation Act 1999.

State of Victoria, Australia
- The Swift Parrot is listed as threatened on the Victorian Flora and Fauna Guarantee Act (1988). Under this Act, an *Action Statement* for the recovery and future management of this species has been prepared.
- On the 2007 advisory list of threatened vertebrate fauna in Victoria, the Swift Parrot is listed as endangered.

Source (edited): "http://en.wikipedia.org/wiki/Swift_Parrot"

Turquoise Parrot

The **Turquoise Parrot** (*Neophema pulchella*) is a parrot previously widespread in Eastern Australia, though now mainly found in northeastern New South Wales and north-eastern Victoria.

A small parrot at around 20 cm long, the male is predominantly green in colour and more yellowish below with a bright turquoise blue face and chestnut shoulders on the blue and green wings. Females are generally duller and paler and lack the chestnut wing patch.

It is found in grasslands and open woodlands, and feeds on grasses, seeds and nectar.

Taxonomy and naming
The English Common Name of the Turquoise Parrot been known alternately as **Chestnut-shouldered parakeet**, **Chestnut-shouldered grass-parakeet**, **Chestnut-shouldered Grass-parrot**, **Chestnut-winged Grass-parakeet**, **Chestnut-winged Grass-Parrot** and **Turquoisine**.

Conservation status

Australia
It is not listed as threatened on the Commonwealth Environment Protection and Biodiversity Conservation Act 1999.

New South Wales
Once common in Western Sydney, it is listed as a Vulnerable species under Schedule 2 of the New South Wales Threatened Species Conservation Act, 1995 (TSC Act).

Victoria
- This species is listed as **threatened** on the Victorian Flora and Fauna Guarantee Act (1988). Under this Act, an *Action Statement* for the recovery and future management of the Turquoise Parrot has not been prepared.
- On the 2007 advisory list of

threatened vertebrate fauna in Victoria, this species is listed as near threatened.

Aviculture

Female

Captive-bred birds adapt readily to aviary conditions, and the species is widely bred. Several colour forms are seen in captivity, including a yellow, red-fronted and pied form (all recessive), and jade and Olive (dominant).

Sundown NP, S.Queensland, Australia

Source (edited): "http://en.wikipedia.org/wiki/Turquoise_Parrot"

Western Ground Parrot

The **Western Ground Parrot** (*Pezoporus flaviventris*) is an endangered species of parrot endemic to Western Australia and is a close relative of the Eastern Ground Parrot (*P. wallicus*) and the somewhat more distantly related and mysterious Night Parrot (*Pezoporus occidentalis*). It is one of the world's rarest birds with about 110 individuals remaining.

The Western Ground Parrot plumage is similar to the Eastern Ground Parrot, but feathers of the abdomen and under tail-coverts are bright yellow with indistinct black barring. The fledgling Western Ground Parrot is grey/brown around the head, wing covets and across the back, while the Eastern Ground Parrot has bright green (adult) plumage in these areas. This plumage difference would provide better camouflage to mobile fledglings in the habitat typical of the southwest arid regions where they reside. In contrast the Eastern Ground Parrot lives in thick vegetation with little open ground.

Molecular DNA evidence suggests the Western Ground Parrot split from Ground Parrots of eastern Australia around 2 million years ago.

Taxonomy

Described as a separate species by Alfred John North in 1911 on account of its distinctive plumage. The specific name, *flaviventris*, is derived from the Latin terms *flavus* "golden-yellow" and *venter* "belly". The Western Ground Parrot was subsequently considered a subspecies of the Eastern Ground Parrot by Gregory Mathews in 1912. He felt it not distinctive enough to warrant specific rank. Other authorities followed suit, until a 2010 molecular study revealed its genetic distinctness from populations in Eastern Australia and Tasmania. The third species in genus is the critically endangered and mysterious Night Parrot (*Pezoporus occidentalis*). The phylogenetic position of the genus Pezoporus within the parrot family remains unclear.

Description

The Western Ground Parrot plumage is similar to the Eastern Ground Parrot (*P. wallicus*), but feathers of the abdomen and under tail-coverts are bright yellow with indistinct black barring. The fledgling Western Ground Parrot is a more neutral grey/brown in colour, while the Eastern Ground Parrot has bright green (adult) plumage in these areas.

Distribution and habitat

Historically, this species was found all along the coast of western southwest Australia from Perth north to Geraldton and along the South Coast east to Israelite Bay. However, it appears to have vanished from the west coast of Western Australia by 1900. Nowadays, the range of this species is limited to two locations along the south coast of Western Australia, east of Albany with the largest population in Cape Arid National Park.

Low heathland usually on deep white

sand with a large diversity of plants is the most common habitat. Parrots appear to be more abundant in heath which has not been burnt for decades, but have been found in areas six years after a burn. There is usually a fairly high component of sedges.

Status

This species is among the rarest bird species in the world. The first photo of the Western Ground Parrot in the wild was taken in 2004. This species has rapidly declined between 1990 and 2009 from about 400 individuals to 110 individuals. Most individuals (~100) are found in the Cape Arid National Park. The species has not yet been evaluated by the IUCN, but it meets several criteria to be considered critically endangered. The main threats are introduced predators, such as foxes and feral cats, as well as wildfires. It is listed as "endangered" by the Australian Government. Much of the local vegetation is vulnerable to *Phytophthora cinnamomi* dieback and it is unclear what impact the loss of certain food items may have on the species.

Behaviour

vocalising

The Western Ground Parrot usually feeds alone or with one other bird. They are rarely seen because they rarely fly or call during daylight, and they are usually hidden among low vegetation. Their plumage offers a good camouflage. If flushed it will fly low over the vegetation, then land again up to 100 or so metres away. Flight when flushed is characterised by a zigzag pattern with short gliding phases and rapid wingbeats. Calling periods are at dusk and early morning before the sun rises; it is a variable high-pitched call audible for some distance and answered by neighbouring members of the species.

Diet

Seeds of various plants especially sedges. e.g. *Mesomaelaena stygia* ssp. *stygia*. Flower buds and the base of flowers e.g. beaufortias, dryandras and grevilleas are also important parts of the diet. A Western Ground Parrot has been observed feeding on the semi-succulent leaves of *Daviesia pachyphylla*. The diet is varied and utilises the high diversity of their habitat.

Breeding

The last nest of the Western Ground Parrot was found in 1913, and was described as a slight depression among low prickly vegetation (possibly the genus *Hakea*) on a low ridge.
Source (edited): "http://en.wikipedia.org/wiki/Western_Ground_Parrot"

Western Rosella

The **Western Rosella** *Platycercus icterotis*, less commonly known as the Stanley Rosella, Earl of Derby's parakeet or Yellow-cheeked parakeet, is the smallest species of rosella and is found in the South West of Australia. in Eucalypt forests and timbered areas. Just under 30 cm (or one foot) long; they are red from the head to the breast with white or beige-ish yellow cheeks and blue and green patterned wings with males being slightly larger and having a more vibrant yellow cheek colouring. Their bills are a grey 'horn' colour like most Australian parrots.

Habitat, Breeding and Diet

Western Rosellas socialise in pairs but will often congregate in largish groups of twenty or so to forage when the season permits; their diet is herbivorous, consisting mostly of grass and seeds. They nest mostly in hollow tree trunks usually a meter or so deep and will favour hollows that have dust in the bottom (as may be created by insects boring out the tree or limb). The female incubates the eggs and leaves in the morning and afternoon to eat food found by the male.

Domestic Rosellas

Western Rosellas make reasonable pets however they have a habit of being aggressive if kept with other pets. They are largely sociable with humans and will whistle in return if whistled at.

Various views and plumages

Western Rosella at Perth Zoo
Source (edited): "http://en.wikipedia.org/wiki/Western_Rosella"

Maroon-bellied Parakeet

The **Maroon-bellied Parakeet** (*Pyrrhura frontalis*) is a small parrot found from southeastern Brazil to north-eastern Argentina, including eastern Paraguay and Uruguay. It is also known as the **Reddish-bellied Parakeet**, and in aviculture it is usually referred to as the **Maroon-bellied Conure**, **Reddish-bellied Conure** or **Brown-eared Conure**.

It has been suggested that the Reddish-bellied Parakeet should include the Blaze-winged Parakeet (*P. devillei*) as a subspecies based on intermediate specimens from Paraguay. But such hybrids are not common in the wild and the two populations generally maintain their integrity; recent sources are undecided on whether to treat them as one species or two.

Description

These birds range from 25 to 28 cm (10–11 in), and are primarily green, with a maroon patch on the belly, a "scaly" yellow-green-barred breast and sides of neck, a whitish ear-patch often tinged brown, and a maroon undertail. The specific name *frontalis* is a reference to its dark maroon frontlet - a feature which separates it from most similar species. The primaries are blue on the outer webs, green on the inner webs, and dark on the tips. The beak is black.

There are two subspecies, with extensive intergradation where their ranges contact:
- **Maroon-bellied Parakeet** proper, *Pyrrhura frontalis frontalis* – Brazil from south Bahia to Rio Grande do Sul, and west to Mato Grosso do Sul. Uppertail greenish-yellow grading into a broad reddish tip.
- **Azara's Conure**, *Pyrrhura frontalis chiripepe* – Eastern Paraguay, Argentina, Uruguay, and far southern Brazil. Uppertail entirely greenish-yellow.

P. f. chiripepe at Cerrito, Rio Grande do Sul, Brazil

Another subspecies, *kriegi*, was described from Bahia in 1932, but today it is universally considered a junior synonym of the nominate subspecies. Distinguished by a narrow brownish-red tip to the tail, it consititutes just a morph or an intermediate genotype making up just 20% of the specimens even in the supposed range. The name **Krieg's Conure** is occasionally used in aviculture for such birds, and some breed them exclusively; they are of course perfectly interfertile with individuals of the normal morph however.

Ecology

The Maroon-bellied Parakeet is common in woodland, and forest edges. In the northern part of its range, it mainly lives in highlands up to 1,400 m (4,600 ft), but elsewhere it is primarily found in lowlands up to 1,000 m (3,300 ft). Tolerates disturbance well and even lives in urban parks (e.g., Rio de Janeiro and São Paulo) and feeds in gardens. Flock size is usually only 6-12 individuals, but up to 40. As other members of the genus *Pyrrhura*, it primarily feeds on fruits, flowers, and similar plant matter; they rarely participate in mixed-species feeding flock..

It is generally common and not considered threatened by the IUCN. Though there is little trade in these parrots, captive-bred birds are occasionally available as pets. Maroon-bellied Parakeets can learn to talk, although not clearly. They are among the quietest conures, but their shrill voices still irritate some people.

Source (edited): "http://en.wikipedia.org/wiki/Maroon-bellied_Parakeet"

Mani the parakeet

Mani the parakeet (hatched 1997), also called **Mani the parrot**, is a Malaysian-born Rose-ringed Parakeet who resides in Singapore. It has been an astrologer 'assistant' to M. Muniyappan since 2005, working from his Little India fortune-telling shop along Serangoon Road. M. Muniyappan is locally known to makes his predictions using a simplified form of cartomancy.

Mani became a celebrity in Singapore, and later internationally, when he picked the correct winners for all of the 2010 FIFA World Cup quarter-final ties, as well as the Spain-Germany semi-final. However, Mani failed to predict the Spain – Netherlands final by choosing Netherlands as the winner of the 2010 World Cup. At one point on July 5, 2010, a day before the Uruguay-Netherlands semi-final match, Mani topped Google's "Hot Searches" in Singapore.

Prior to his World Cup stint, Mani and his owner M. Muniyappan, used to see an average of 10 customers a day. Following his World Cup success, this increased to around 10 customers an hour.

Predictions

Fortune tellers with parakeets are a common sight in Singapore's Little India. Here, owner M. Muniyappan sits with Mani the Parakeet.

While Mani typically assisted his owner Muniyappan in fortune-telling in day-to-day work, it was his predictions over the matches of the 2010 FIFA World Cup that saw him gain widespread recognition.

According to Singapore's The New Paper, Mani's most contentious pick for the World Cup thus far was underdog Netherlands to beat Brazil. His prediction later proved to be correct.

The quarter-finals saw Mani guessing the four winners of the matches correctly – Spain, Germany, Uruguay and Netherlands. In the semi-finals, he predicted that Uruguay would beat Netherlands and Spain would defeat Germany, thereby leading to a Uruguay vs Spain final. Mani went on further to predict that Spain would be champions.

The Uruguay vs Netherlands prediction turned out to be wrong, with Netherlands progressing on to the final. As a result, Mani made a new prediction for the World Cup Final between Netherlands and Spain. It tipped a Dutch win over Spain. On the other hand, fellow oracle star Paul the Octopus of Germany went for a Spanish victory, resulted in some media outlets describing the game as an octopus-versus-parakeet showdown. However, Spain defeated the Netherlands 1-0 and Paul was proven to be triumphant.

Method of divination

Mani exits his small wooden cage and chooses between two white cards — each hiding the flag of the countries of a match that will be played. Mani will pick one of the cards up with his beak and flip it over, revealing the winner for the match. Some Singaporeans, in particular older generations, seek fortune tellers for advice.

Following his successful stint in predicting the semi-finalists of the World Cup, Mani rose to international stardom. The New Paper of Singapore was the first to feature his story and predictions, and newspapers from across the globe soon followed suit – partially as a result of *The New Paper*'s frequent broadcast on the bird. News agencies including the AFP and Associated Press ran reports on Mani, alongside newspapers such as The Guardian, the Daily Mail, and American magazine Vanity Fair.

Mani's story is closely aligned with that of Paul the Octopus, who has maintained 100% accuracy in its predictions for Germany in the FIFA World Cup 2010. The World Cup final saw some media outlets terming it as more of a Octopus vs Parakeet showdown, with the two having chosen opposing teams. Paul the Octopus emerged the winner in the psychic showdown.

Source (edited): "http://en.wikipedia.org/wiki/Mani_the_parakeet"